Triumph T120/T140
Bonneville

Great
Bikes

Triumph T120/T140

Bonneville

Steve Wilson *Foreword by Hughie Hancox*

First published in 2000

A catalogue record for this book is available from the British Library

ISBN 1 85960 679 2

Library of Congress catalog card no. 00-134246

Published by Haynes Publishing, Sparkford,
Nr Yeovil, Somerset BA22 7JJ, England

Tel. 01963 442030 Fax 01963 440001
Int. tel. +44 1963 442030 Fax +44 1963 440001
E-mail: sales@haynes-manuals.co.uk
Web site: www.haynes.co.uk

Haynes North America, Inc.,
861 Lawrence Drive, Newbury Park,
California 91320, USA

Printed and bound in England by J. H. Haynes & Co. Ltd, Sparkford

Contents

Acknowledgements

This book owes a great deal to the generosity, with their time and knowledge, of my ex-Meriden friends, starting with Hughie Hancox, and including particularly John Nelson. I should also like to thank Bob Haines, Bob Innes, Bill Crosby and John South for their unstinting co-operation. The Triumph Owners Club folk were very helpful too.

John Nelson was also kind enough to supply original contemporary photographs. Cyril Ayton, late of *Motor Cycle Sport*, and again Bob Haines and John South, also provided pictures, as did *The Classic Motor Cycle*, by whose kind permission the cutaway engine drawings are reproduced.

But 'main man' with the lens was Garry Stuart, who took all the original illustrations of restored Bonnies which so thoroughly enhance this book. As ever, it has been both a privilege and a pleasure to work with the tireless and resourceful Garry.

The owners of the beautifully restored machines were equally unfailingly generous with their pride and joys, and with their time. I must start with Don Taylor, who let me loose on his superb 1970 T120, as described in Chapter 1.

Robert Powell also let me have a go on his '63, as did Mark Bradley on his '71 oil-in-framer. Yorkshireman Terry McDonald gave us free run of his amazing collection, and once again Bill Crosby at the London Motorcycle Museum lent invaluable help with his T140s, as did Roy Swainbank, and Tony Miller of Miller Motorcycles, Hastings. John Vernon's beautiful pre-units were a high spot, as were Keith Barnett's T120TT, Graham Bowen's T120RT and Martin Bartlett's T140 US Royal Wedding. Every one was a winner. Also Julian Vockins' cover bike.

In Chapter 5, the tale of John and Jane South's travels on a Bonnie appeared in a different form in No 8 of the now defunct *Silver Machine* magazine; and a longer version of the interview with Bob Haines was published in *Classic Bike Guide* No 111, and is reproduced here by kind permission of the editor.

Last and not least, for their patience I should like to thank Darryl Reach, Flora Myer and Alison Roelich at Haynes Publishing, and also my wife Molly at home. And finally, a special 'thank you' to Bernie Cochran, who heroically hammered the keyboard when she wasn't feeling very well at all.

Glossary of abbreviations

bhp	brake horsepower
CBG	*Classic Bike Guide* magazine
HP	hire-purchase
ISDT	International Six-Days Trial
MCN	*Motor Cycle News*, weekly paper
o-i-f	oil-in-frame – oil-bearing motorcycle chassis
pre-unit	engine with separate gearbox
qd	quickly detachable (rear wheel)
rpm	revolutions per minute
sls	single leading shoe (drum brake)
TDC	top dead centre
tls	twin leading shoe (drum brake)
UNF	Unified Finescrew thread
unit	engine and gearbox made as one unit
VMCC	Vintage Motor Cycle Club

Foreword

by Hughie Hancox

Being asked to write this foreword has a special meaning for me, because after completing my National Service and returning to work at Meriden, I was seconded to the Experimental Department.

At this particular time, extensive mileage at very high speeds was being carried out on the then prototype high-performance machine, which we in the department lovingly called the 'Monster'. I don't think the name 'Bonneville' had yet been thought up – this would come later, as a flash of inspiration, and also as a timeless salute to that stretch of salt flat in Utah.

The 'Monster' was in fact a Crystal-grey 1958 Tiger 110, equipped with the parts from that year's high-performance kit, plus a little bit of secret 'know-how'. This kept Percy Tait, chief experimental tester, just that little bit quicker than anyone else he happened to come up against during his runs, often in excess of 100mph, up and down the A1 road and the local highways – the M1 motorway would not be opened until the following year – and that included the local constabularies through whose territories he passed.

Down through the years since its introduction, the Bonneville has carved a special niche which it has made exclusively its own. No other mass-produced machine has been so immortalised, indeed, all the world and its uncle seems to have owned a Bonneville at some time or another. As long as Meriden is remembered and spoken of at Triumph gatherings, the word Bonneville will always figure largely in conversations, and quite rightly so.

When asked if I would write this foreword, I must say I was honoured. Having helped Steve on Volumes 5 and 6 of his earlier work on classic British motorcycles, I know he is eminently knowledgeable on this subject – even though he has this peculiar bent/tendency towards the Meriden sister company's products from Small Heath. Nevertheless, he is more than qualified to do justice to this publication in celebration of the Bonneville.

Hughie Hancox
Coventry, May 2000

Introduction

Your first thought will almost certainly be the same as mine was: *another* book about Bonnevilles?

Starting with John Nelson's definitive development history, there have now been several excellently detailed studies of this charismatic, immensely popular motorcycle. First among equals would have to be American David Gaylin's shame-makingly thorough *Triumph Motorcycle Restoration Guide: Bonneville and TR6*, but Roy Bacon's *Triumph Twin Restoration* and Gerard Kane's *Original Triumph Bonneville* are also worthy contenders. I've even contributed myself, in Volume 6 of *British Motorcycles since 1950*. So why another Bonnie book?

Because the magic lives on. A combination of mass production and design/engineering flair branded the Triumph T120, the 650 Bonnie, into the very soul of more than one age group of riders, on more than one continent. 'The Power of British Engineering, the Glory of American Styling', as BSA/Triumph Group publicity put it at one point, but the matter was more complex than that, the interaction of US and English dreams and achievements which forged the Bonnie's inimitable style, the model's historical integrity. This Triumph was a unique fusion of Anglo-America: its cutting edge character was often in fact the product of tension between the two cultures.

So yes, although the nuts and bolts of the Bonneville's organic development have been well documented, a machine that was nothing less than a cultural icon can always be celebrated anew. By a happy accident, it looks

as though this book will appear shortly after an all-new parallel twin bearing the Bonneville name has been launched by Hinckley Triumph; a Bonnie for the new millennium, proof in itself of the abiding power of the name.

I hope this work is not short on detail, but its prime purpose is as a celebration of a real 'people's machine', a bike that won on the tracks and in the dirt but more importantly, won the hearts and minds of at least one generation of motorcyclists, the rebel boys and girls who, as Bruce Springsteen sang, 'learned more from a three-minute record/Than they ever did in school'.

I've learned a few things myself while writing it, and I hope even the most knowledgeable enthusiast will find something to amuse, instruct or bedazzle in these pages, not least in the magnificent spread of colour photos by lens wizard Garry Stuart.

So, drop the coin right into the slot, and let's roll!

Steve Wilson
Fawler, Oxon
May 2000

Two greats: Mike Hailwood on his 1968 Triumph Bonneville.

A lion in winter

A January day in Malvern, with the tracery of interlaced boughs on the bare trees hanging like smoke in the beautiful hills above the town. Winter cold, but I don't think about it. I am about to ride a legend.

Let me explain a little. As a young rider in the 1960s and '70s, I had come up on Norton's 350, 500, 650 and 750 twins, then shifted gradually to 650 BSAs. There was a 'Big Three' in British bike terms, and the third (and largest) had been Triumph. But it had been no coincidence that the only Triumph twin I had ever owned had been a unit 350 bought to sell on, which I had done, quickly.

Today, the notion of marque loyalty is rather different from the way it was then. Now that there are no bad bikes (so we're told) most of the fierceness has gone out of the arguments. The equivalent to the way Triumph was until 1970, the best known, best selling, best all-round marque, must be Honda, and if you're a Honda man you're probably one for life. True, lovers of the latest race rep may hop and swap makes, but riders who have discovered the perennial and versatile Honda VFR will be likely to look no further – which had been the way it was with Triumph twins. The same is true, for different reasons, of BMW pilots and Harley-Davidson men. But few of them claim superiority at the expense of equivalent rivals, as BSA, Norton and Triumph fans were prone to do. Once, in the early Sixties, a young Triumph wannabe whom I knew, came up to me in a pub and said, 'I don't like your Norton's front brake'. He looked ready to fight about it.

It was a subject with complex roots. At my Oxford college, for instance, there was a Velocette, a 250 Royal Enfield, a couple of scooters and two of us with Nortons, but no Triumphs at all. We cannot avoid the C-word; class was a factor, no question, and the 650 Bonneville in particular was fundamentally a working class hero. Part of the reason was simple economics – in 1962 its real rival on the streets of Britain, the Norton 650SS, cost £351, while a T120 Bonnie was £309. That £42 difference represented nearly a month's money in those days. Edward Turner's tightly run ship at Meriden produced affordable sports performance. Norton twins were also much scarcer, partly due to their peerless Featherbed frames being made in restricted numbers by Reynolds Tubes, and they tended to be bought by more mature riders.

No doubt some sober enthusiasts rode and enjoyed their T120s responsibly, but they didn't get the public's attention like the swarthy Brylcreemed delinquents with pock-marked complexions, greased leathers and bad attitudes, the ones ever-ready with vee-signs that had nothing to do with victory. It was evidently the same in the States, where the vast majority of Bonnevilles in the Sixties, the glory days, would be sold.

Columnist Maynard Hershon wrote recently of his first bike, a '62 CB72 Honda 250, 'the bike that introduced big-bike motorcycling to clean-cut America … we'd never known anyone who rode a motorcycle … We certainly could not afford the price of admission to HD or BSA-Triumph style motorcycling. We didn't want to give up button-down shirts or khaki pants …

You could own a Hawk and not establish a relationship with the scary-looking guy who fixed bikes …' But to the wild ones (had it all started with Brando's 650 Thunderbird?), and the tattooed hoods, Triumphs were cool, and 40-cube Bonnevilles were very low temperature indeed.

On both sides of the Atlantic, then, 650 Bonnies were for bad boys; they were the business, the outer limit, the dark side. Which may explain some of the animosity between riders of what were essentially quite similar designs of motorcycles – all were large capacity parallel twins. That rivalry was one paradox; another was that despite their tough aura, Bonnevilles were in fact the lightest, most elegant and even daintiest of all the big twins, they were *reet petite*. 'Bonnie'– the word itself is both a female name – down home, a little wild – with also the Scots connotation of a lively, heart-warming prettiness. As one rider put it, 'they were very feminine – but all us butch berks wanted one'.

But the ones who didn't had some valid ammunition during the long arguments over scarred coffee bar tables. BSA twin riders, especially in the pre-unit era, could point out that their engines were sturdier and wore out much slower than Triumph's – and they were right. While Norton men knew that their Featherbed frame provided handling in a class of its own, a world away from Triumph's 'instant whip' swinging arm chassis as found on the pre-unit Bonnies – and they were right too. The vastly experienced rider and road-test journalist Dave Minton wrote the following with feeling:

'… the frame saddle tube, on which the swinging arm pivot was mounted, warped like a torsion bar and gave fast cornering a horrible new meaning entirely … If you ever want to frighten yourself, give an early swinging fork 650 Triumph lash around a mountain road.' And yet, Dave Minton's classic bike is a Triumph twin, and it didn't stop those early Bonnies selling like hot cakes. Ex-Meriden Service Manager John Nelson has confirmed that handling troubles rarely cropped up as a service problem, and the truth is that the flaw, although real enough, could be mastered by a skilled and determined rider, as well as compensated for by the Bonnie's tuneability for speed and by its lightness. The liability actually became a warped virtue, a badge of pride. 'Triumphs don't handle?' Then how come you end up so often eating their dust?

As we shall see, it was all change for 1963 when Doug Hele and his team, newly arrived from Norton, set about transforming the Bonnie's chassis at the same time as the engine became a unit ie with the motor and gearbox built in a common housing. Ironically, the British rockers, caff society, you might say, didn't care much for the new, more compact engine arrangement. But by then the whole game, too, was changing. After an all-time peak in 1959, motorcycle sales in Britain plummeted disastrously from 1960 and would remain low throughout the decade. The reasons were two-fold: government withdrawal after election success of the short-term economic incentives, of which the main one had been a low hire-purchase rate; and more fundamentally, increasing affluence coupled with a new generation of affordable, peppy motorcars spearheaded by the Mini. This became the realistic transport choice for the vast majority of young people, as well as the previously numerous sidecar brigade. Motorcycling was changed, famously, from mainly primary transport to leisure activity. In conjunction with this, although the cars might be British for a while, the smart money, which included the Mods, by 1961 had recognised what we all take for granted now: that it was time to stop talking about the war. It was recognised that Japanese technological skills, along with production machinery new after 1945, had combined with their total focus to produce consumer durables with previously unimaginable standards of performance and reliability. Could it be long before big motorcycles joined the ranks of these products?

Meanwhile, Meriden soldiered on, partly with belt-driven machinery retrieved in 1940 from their bombed-out Coventry factory. (Did you know that 'knocking off' work referred to knocking the belt off its drive at the end of the day?) The rockers were reduced to a dwindling sub-culture, and an increasingly unfashionable

A UK unit T120 for 1966. They handled.

one, while the main action shifted to the other side of the pond. By the mid-Sixties, Triumph, as part of the BSA Group which had taken it over in 1951, were exporting 85 per cent of their motorcycles, and 80 per cent of that export total was going to North America. In the short-term, this was possible because, since the war, Edward Turner had built up an excellent, well-supported dealer network there. Taking a longer view, the Bonneville, strange but true, was in the right place at the right time, a sporty, charismatic all-rounder there in place to surf the post-war 'Baby Boom'. The Sixties, as the poet observed, began in 1963, which a) just happened to be the year when the Unit T120 was launched, and b) was around the time when the first of the wartime population explosion could afford wheels of their own. Came the hour, came the Bonneville.

Why Triumph, and not so much the other two Great British marques? God, as usual, was on the side of the big battalions. Nortons were marketed by the East Coast-based Berliner brothers and anyway, never produced enough Featherbed-framed twins to do serious business. From 1968 Commandos would redress this somewhat and prove popular on the West Coast, but in 10 years of production,

only around 60,000 of these twins in both 750 and 850 form would be built. BSA was a more serious contender, with a factory capable, in theory, of producing up to 75,000 motorcycles a year. But while their pre-unit twins had been both popular and well-respected, their A65 unit 650s from 1962 on, were neither. They were saddled with somewhat featureless 'power egg' engines, which Edward Turner, as head of the BSA Group's Automotive Division, had helped to lay out. Leaving aside the economic arguments for unit construction, could their lacklustre styling have been Turner's oblique way of making Triumphs look even better? Although the short-stroke BSAs would prove quite reliable and durable motorcycles once their electrics had been sorted out, and later variants such as the Lightning Clubman and export Spitfire were quite good-looking, despite the efforts of dedicated individuals at BSA, they failed to benefit from the concentrated effort of an equivalent to Doug Hele's Experimental Department at Meriden. So they never really shook off the stigma of the 'watermelon engines', as contemptuous American Triumph men dubbed the unit BSA twin motors. Some 90,000 A65s would be built in all.

Contrast that with the Bonneville. According

American beauty: the 1966 T120TT, US export personified.

to Triumph's then Marketing Director, Ken Chambers, approximately 250,000 had been built by December 1972, and subsequent production by the Meriden co-op rounded the figure out to about 300,000 (out of some 850,000 Triumph twins of all types built since 1956).

No wonder, then, that 'Bonneville' became a household word among young American gearheads. As in the UK, there were relatively subtle but very definite divisions among the Sixties motorcycling fraternity. Hershon gives another example, relating to the two versions of Honda's 305cc Super Hawk. 'High-school athletes bought Scramblers. Guys who didn't fit in bought Hawks.'

The Bonneville crowd was something else altogether. One fastidious owner of two beautifully restored pre-units whom we met, had only come to motorcycling just a few years previously. He told us how, after getting going on modern machinery, to his credit he began to take to the road on his T120s. 'Then I was in the house one day and I thought, hang on, what's that smell? Oil, petrol … It took a while to realise it was *me*.' Yes, Bonneville ownership affected every area of your life.

A 1970 UK T120 in the Malvern Hills.

A *Cycle World* test also observed in passing that 'the half-stud, half-racing "Bonneville image" is the very thing that has kept (the Triumph) firm alive and well to this date'. America's *Cycle* magazine too said of the Bonneville: 'Spend some time with this prince among two-wheelers … and you'll come to understand why it's been around so long … what it (has) is great mechanical presence … the big Bonneville is one of the two or three most *desirable* motorcycles being made in the world today.'

That was written in 1969, one of the T120's peak years, and while the model was by then well-sorted and the sentiments were evidently sincere, on the other side of the pond, this writer at 26 years of age never considered a Bonneville for a moment. My eyes were firmly fixed on a Norton 750 Commando, the natural successor to the 650SS I was running then. My loss, no doubt, but that was how deep marque loyalty and prejudice ran on this thorny subject.

Since then, as a road tester for *Classic Bike Guide* and other magazines, over the years my views have shifted on Triumph twins. I have found out how truly, unbelievably smooth an expertly rebuilt early 650 6T Thunderbird can be, far more so than any other British twin I had encountered; Triumph's later reputation for maximum shakes masked the fact that in the 1940s and '50s, they had been considered famously civilised power plants. I discovered what a workhorse a nice old pre-unit 5T could be, and how well a ground-up rebuilt, judiciously tweaked T140 Bonneville could go. But the prejudice lingered, even if 'Triumphs don't handle' gave way to the more mature sounding 'Triumphs aren't as durable'. And somehow, I had never got around to the heart of the matter; the 1963–70 unit twins with Doug Hele's imprint on their performance and handling, plus a style gradually refined and matured; a design classic, if you will.

So, no classic Bonneville ride, until that morning in Malvern. Thanks to a generous collector, there sat a fully restored UK-spec 1970 T120R. The owner warned me that it had not been run for a while, and then let me get on with it. Tickle the twin Concentric carbs, switch on the ignition key, which since 1968 had been

handily placed on the left side of the fork cover, and halfway down the first kick, the Bonnie burst into life. An essential part of being an easy bike to ride is starting like that.

Moving off on damp roads on an industrial estate, we soon passed the surviving works of another Great British automotive institution,

Morgan cars; many felt that a well-built and subtly updated Bonneville could have survived even today in the same way as Morgan had – a cherished anachronism. Meanwhile the actual icon I was riding was making music, and it wasn't Elgar. The first few miles through town were lumpy, grumpy, with the engine coughing and missing on the throttle, with low speed shakes so heavy you could call them quakes. This was a bad mo'sickle, yet somehow I sensed that the bike was just getting itself together after a long sleep and that soon enough it would clear its throat. Meanwhile, strangely, it still felt good and tractable at low speeds and in the traffic, genuinely easy to ride.

The back brake wasn't much use, but the front 8in twin leading shoe design, probably the best-ever British production drum brake, more than compensated. The clutch was light and the gearchange from the unit box never less than clean, with neutral easy to find even at a standstill. The owner, who was smaller than I, had tilted the wideish swept-back handlebars up slightly, so that the ends dug into my palms, but I soon forgot about it and found I could tiller the bike around the bends with the bars very effectively. As I got clear of the town's outskirts and headed on to the twisting road which climbed up and along the flanks of the Malvern Hills, the steering proved truly excellent, with no white-lining or getting knocked off line by holes or patches in the road.

The engine did settle down, and it felt … *beefy*. It liked to go, there was a constant feeling of controlled urge, of banked-back rage. Bend-swinging up and down the hills – well, Norton's Featherbed may have had that utter predictability, but this wasn't half bad, and both forks and frame offered a more supple, and much more forgiving ride than the harshness which had always been the penalty for the Norton's excellence. This 650 was not a revvy motor like Triumph's unit 500, but it did help if you kept it above 3,000rpm. With the hillside bends coming thick and fast, you changed down for engine braking – yes! chasing the power. Acceleration, on this example at least, was not startling but it was constant, seamless, with no power step. And all the time it wanted to Go!

After 10 miles or so, I took a turning I recognised and followed another wonderfully twisty road back towards Tewkesbury. By this time I had realised that this Bonnie was not giving of its best at the top end. The Smith's magnetic speedo was as erratic as they usually were – not for nothing did police Triumphs fit calibrated versions of the previous chronometric instruments – wavering between 75 and 85 when there should have been up to 20mph more. A quick glance at the mileometre told the tale – just 710 miles recorded, which proved to be all it had done since the rebuild.

In a way, however, that made me appreciate the Bonnie's all-rounder character even more. We reeled off a few more tip-tilting miles with the T120's firm suspension maybe no comfort aid, but certainly a big help when taking fast bends on a rising throttle. On reflection, comfort from the quilt-topped seat and the upright riding position was good, but I was not to think about that until after the exhilarating ride was done. Then, turning off into the walled lane by Eastnor Castle, the Triumph proved willing to poddle gently around the narrow winding road and creep past a horse and rider before accelerating away through the incredibly slick gearbox. I appreciated the box more with every twisting, swooping mile; along with the well-chosen ratios which allowed available power to be exploited right through the range. It would even snick into 1st every time, not something for which Triumphs were famous. At one brief stop, the centre-stand proved very easy to use. As the sky darkened I reached forward and flicked on the headlamp-mounted light switch, an excellently easy and accessible arrangement. One absent-minded car driver in a side turning required a light touch of the legendary dual Windtone horns – which proved seriously loud, as loud as a car horn, and startled me as much as they did him – surely a British biking first! In many little details, this was

This 1970 Bonnie's owner puts his machine through its paces.

a real rider's motorcycle.

But it was the rise and fall of the stirring deep noise from the engine, as the excellent handling was pitted against the undulating curves of the hill and valley road, which stole the day, especially with the security of a brake which could either feather off speed when needed or pin you right back in an emergency. This Bonnie wasn't particularly good climbing the longer hills in top; it would not have been an outstanding fast tourer like the Commando. It was a sports bike through and through, and one remembered hearing that, unlike a BSA or Norton which liked to be ridden two-up, the Triumph gave of its best when ridden solo. What it gave, above all, was exhilaration.

That flexible free-revving motor called to mind the chorus of LaBelle's song 'Lady Marmalade' – 'More! More! More!' – and in another way too, for tantalisingly, you felt it could be even smoother, even quicker etc and if it was yours, you would constantly be tempted to fine-tune, tweak and refine it. That too was another aspect of the deep involvement Bonnevilles required, another reason why people loved them.

Back at my generous friend's base there were a couple of other typical Triumph experiences. Looking the engine over revealed a healthy spattering of oil on the crankcase top behind the cylinders. Oops! But then again, the 1970 bike was *wonderful* just to look at. The short, fat silencers, the chromed-rimmed 'picture-frame' tank badge with its black 'Triumph' on a pebbled silver background, the elegantly slanted script of the gold 'Bonneville' side panel transfer, the so-compact engine with the fluted cover to break up the primary chaincase, and the taut 62° head angle and high-mounted chrome headlamp shell helping lift and thrust forward the machine's profile. Even the Astral Red UK petrol tank with its gold-lined silver panels

which one US writer had judged 'only a mother could love', turned out to be just fine in the cellulose and metal. It was a truly aesthetic pleasure. Form following function but with style, and I had to admit it beat hands down, even the export A65s (which I like) with their dumpy silencers, banana-shaped tanks and, yes, watermelon engines.

It is no wonder, then, that Bonnevilles, pre-unit and unit 650s, plus T140 750s, today still make very good prices. The only exception are the 1971–73 oil-in-frame 650s, the machines which followed the year after the so-excellent bike I had just ridden and which in one disastrous stroke heralded the twilight of the Bonneville street Gods; a *Gutterdamerung* of famous proportions which tars those bikes still. Otherwise it is completely understandable that middle-aged men should want to rediscover that vivid excitement which a Bonneville could kindle like few other motorcycles.

The trouble is, you can fit a fabric-covered wiring harness to your T120, plus new/old stock Lodge or KLG spark plugs just like the original, and in the UK, you can even buy a replica road tax disc from the year your Triumph was made. But the youth, the quick blood – where do you source that? Still, if any mechanical artefact can offer instant rejuvenation, it is probably the sight, sound and feel of a well-sorted Bonnie.

So, how did it all get started?

The perfected twin. Note the Windtone horns.

'100 miles an hour standing still' – the 1961 T120 now looked like the roadburner it was.

Birth of the Bonnie:
The pre-unit T120s

Nineteen fifty-eight was a good year for the Triumph Engineering Company at Meriden.

This was the 21st anniversary of Edward Turner's ground-breaking 500T Speed Twin, the machine which, in 1937, had single-handedly set the course of the British motorcycle industry for the following four decades.

The previous year, 1957, had seen the 21st birthday for the Triumph Engineering Company itself. This enterprise had been formed in 1936 when Turner's mentor, Jack Sangster, bought the motorcycle side of the old Triumph Motor Company Ltd, which concentrated on four wheels from then on. Sangster had appointed Turner as both Chief Designer and General Manager of the new motorcycle outfit, and from then on the company had never looked back.

Even the destruction of its Priory Street

'From a Buick 6' – the mouth-organ tank badge – an early case of American influence.

factory during the 1940 Blitz of Coventry had worked for Triumph, as it had led to the move in 1942 to a purpose-built factory in a green-field site at the village of Meriden, mid-way between Coventry and Birmingham. Although there was an (inconclusive) official enquiry as to how Sangster had swung this, when most of the rest of the industry had remained confined, post-war, to their existing antiquated industrial premises in Plumstead and Birmingham.

Turner was in every sense the company's presiding genius. The great designer, Bert Hopwood, who would play a dour Laurel to Turner's effervescent Hardy throughout their careers, recalled ET declaring at one point that he, Turner, was 'the Works Manager, the Sales Manager, the General Manager and the buyer!' He certainly liked control, and this included control over the number of machines Meriden produced, even when there was constant public demand for more. By the late 1950s, around 1,100 workers were building about 28,000 motorcycles a year, including some 10,000 of the entry-level Tiger Cub 200 singles – all the rest were twins. And Turner also dictated what kind of bikes they were to be.

Since pre-war days he had grasped the potential of the North American market, and the Fifties had been ushered in with the 6T Thunderbird, a bored and stroked 650 version of the 500 twin, particularly aimed at the long highways of the USA; although also at sidecar

'Win on Sunday, Sell on Monday' – Eddie Mulder hard-charging a pre-unit Bonnie in a desert enduro.

men in the UK where outfits represented one in three big bikes on the road. The Thunderbird name was an early, inspired example of US influence, although Turner had not gone to its source in native American mythology, but on his way to the races at Daytona, Florida, had spotted the name on a South Carolina motel. American thinking would permeate the product – the '57-on archetypal 'mouth organ' big chromed tank badge consciously echoed the radiator grille of a Buick automobile.

Turner's contract specified that he should spend six months of each year in the USA, where he helped build up a formidable dealer network complete with training schools and dealer conventions, based both in the West,

(the 19 states west of the eastern border of Texas) at JoMo or Johnson Motors, Pasadena, California, and the East, where more bikes would always be sold via expatriate Dennis MacCormack of the wholly-owned subsidiary of TriCor, or Triumph Corp Inc in Baltimore. These would provide a sound basis for expansion when the trickle of Triumphs (1,000 a year in 1950) became a flood in the 1960s.

Like Triumph and their owners BSA, the giant manufacturing Group and motorcycle makers which had bought the Meriden company from Sangster in 1951, the East and West Coast organisations became bitter rivals, but meanwhile American sales increased daily, and often on the basis of 'Win on Sunday, Sell on

Monday'. Many dealerships raced what they sold. Sports successes, at Daytona, on flat tracks and in desert cross-country events, fuelled Triumph's popularity among young Americans. Although the track success was mainly with 500s, as historian Tim Remus pointed out, 'Americans on the street always seem to prefer the larger 650 twins'. For motorcycles in the States, sports action rather than ride-to-work or touring was then overwhelmingly the name of the game.

That, however, was not Edward Turner's view of the two-wheel scene, and many of Triumph's greatest hits, the Bonneville included, came about almost in spite of, rather than because of, their boss. He had early decided that European-type road racing was an expensive blind alley for a motorcycle manufacturer, resulting in 'nothing that can be translated into production'. He had a point, as Dr Joseph Kelly remarked in his memoirs, 'when Norton were supreme in the racing world, the Ariel Red Hunter outsold the Model 18 Norton by two to one, and the Triumph Speed Twin outsold it by three to one.'

Turner did endorse off-road competition, in the enduro-style ISDT, as well as in trials and the increasingly popular scrambles/motocross, considering it provided more relevant feedback for production roadsters than road racing ever could. At Meriden there was a small, under-funded Competition Department overseen by Henry Vale. It was there, however, as well as at 'Baker's Corner', where the brilliant tuner Frank Baker presided over what could loosely be described as product development, that Turner's intentions were subverted. Hot competition machinery was brewed, and the source of many of the tuning parts for it was, not unnaturally, the USA.

Despite Turner having been a Brooklands man and a road racer pre-war, this really was at odds with his thinking as he approached his 60th year. Triumph's 21st had been celebrated by the 350cc Twenty-One/3TA with its unit construction engine and 'bath tub' rear panelling. This was the nearest Turner could get to the dream, exemplified by his earlier 3TU prototype, of an Everyman motorcycle with full enclosure, just like the Continental scooters, which in the late 1950s in the UK were outselling motorcycles by three to two. The enclosed Triumphs, with their well-chosen two-tone colour schemes, started an industry trend of less elegant imitation; it turned out to be a blind alley, and the panelling on Triumphs was deeply unpopular in America. On both sides of the Atlantic, in fact, boys would be boys, and what the boys wanted was stripped-down racer looks and power, plenty of power.

So the hot camshaft grinds, gas-flowed cylinder heads, specially wound valve springs, and more, made their way to Meriden, often while the US subsidiary's Competition and Service Department folk were visiting. As far back as 1955, Henry Vale's scrambles ace Johnny Giles and others in Britain had been using on their 650s an adapted alloy twin carburettor cylinder head from the Tiger 100 race kit. On the off-roaders this was not fitted for the extra top end it provided, but to bypass the frame's rear downtube, which had prevented the fitting of a fibre head spacer or a large air filter reservoir to the single carb machine, to improve the breathing and hence give the 650s the low-down torque they needed on the dirt.

Power had also got a boost on the 1957 Delta alloy head 650 T110, and new petrol additives were permitting higher compression ratios. All this, coupled with the increased popularity of production racing in the UK, had overstressed the existing 650's three-piece crankshaft. Early in 1958, Meriden's Chief Designer, Charles Grandfield, instituted a test-bed project for a one-piece forged crank, with a bolt-on flywheel. To get the necessary power for its evaluation, a modified Tiger 100 splayed-inlet twin carb cylinder head was fitted to a T110. And as the book accompanying the Guggenheim's Art of the Motorcycle exhibition correctly observed, 'twin carburettors … defined the Bonneville'.

Now twin carburettors were seen by many as a decidedly mixed blessing. They were both thirstier and fussier than a single instrument, one more thing to go wrong, and needed care, time and again, to get both instruments in balance. They did, however, allow for wilder valve timing. With cams like the race-bred

E3134 keeping the valves open longer, and an optional three-keyway valve-timing set-up allowing you to time accordingly, the last ounce of power could be extracted at the top end. The very top end, in the case of Johnny Allen's 1956 streamliner which, at Bonneville Flats, Utah, took the *de facto* motorcycle World Speed Record at 214.47mph (345.08kph), powered by a heavily modified Triumph 650 with twin carburettors. That was the headline-grabber, but Gary Richards' Class C records on an unfaired T120 – 149.51mph (240.56kph) in 1960, then 159.54mph (256.7kph) in 1961 – were even better for American throttle-jockeys to identify with. For record-breaking and racing, twin carbs were fine, and Meriden issued a Technical Bulletin (TIB) detailing preparation and engine assembly, the three-keyway valve timing included, for production racing. The aim was to maximise the inlet gas charge time, but then prevent its premature loss from the combustion chamber by altering the exhaust timing overlap. But top restorer Hughie Hancox was not alone in believing that 'for the ordinary bloke the benefit was nil. I didn't bother with it. We always knew a bloody good TR6 (the "single carb Bonneville") on the road would give the Bonnie a run for it's money.'

This, however, true as it was, ignores one crucial factor. Those jutting twin carbs were a highly visible go-faster badge, a feature that at one stroke defined the rider out of the ranks of the sensible and over towards the 'too-fast-to-live-too-young-to-die' rebels. For as the Sixties' American Champion racer Gene 'Burrito' Romero wrote: 'Like those who rode and raced them, Triumph had an aura as rebels'. It had to be a Bonneville.

Back in 1958, however, there was still Edward Turner's cautious reluctance to overcome. This was attacked in several ways. According to Service Manager and later

The headlamp nacelle, with Rev-o-lator speedo, made the early Bonnie a hybrid.

definitive historian of the model, John Nelson, the experimental twin carb T110, in a bid to appeal to ET's aesthetic instincts, got the Show treatment. Although Hancox, then working in the Service Department, confirms that the bike was finished in standard T110 silver grey. 'We used to call it "the Monster"' Hughie recalled. 'Alan Gillingham and I used to work on it. Percy Tait (Experimental's main tester as well as Triumph's top Production racer) would take it up to Apex Corner and back again before lunch, and while he was in the canteen, Alan and I would check it over for his afternoon stint. Then, when Percy would come back again at four, we'd get it on the bench and check it from front to back, readying it for the following morning. The Bonneville was a natural derivative of the twin carb T110.' Tait's road-test programme highlighted some specific weak points revealed by the engine's high output. Its clutch became over-stressed, and as a result all 1959 clutches would have a different grade of friction material.

The 'Monster' may have been in standard T110 colours, but Nelson wrote that, unlike the usual deliberately undistinguished and disguised pre-production prototypes, Experimental chief Frank Baker, who was firmly in the go-faster camp, had made sure that it had been built 'with full Paint and Polishing Shop participation', to tickle Turner's undoubted eye for the aesthetically pleasing. Features of which the boss was proud, such as the five-bar tank-top parcel grid and the shapely, tidy headlamp nacelle, were still reassuringly there (despite the fact that the headlamp cowling dictated that the legs of the spindly 'inside spring' forks remained close set, and that cable runs through it were less than ideal) – but in combination with things like the short, dropped-angle handlebars and GP remote float for the carbs, all of which screamed 'Speed'!

Other factors were also at work on ET. In 1957, after Jack Sangster had succeeded in ousting the Group's Chairman Sir Bernard Docker in the sort of reverse takeover of BSA at boardroom level, Edward Turner had been appointed Chief of the Group's Automotive Division, encompassing Daimler cars as well as Ariel and BSA motorcycles. Perhaps this helped take his eye off the ball long enough for the go-fast conspirators to get as far as they did! But it also brought him into contact with sports bikes from BSA, which despite his responsibility for them, would paradoxically always remain the chief rivals of 'his' Triumphs. There were the highly developed Gold Star singles, which although anachronisms in the age of twin cylinders, were real racers-with-lights and had, embarrassingly for Triumph, proved the point from 1955 to 1957 in the new and popular Thruxton 9-hour Production races. Goldies had taken overall victory in both 500 and even 350 guise, leaving the Meriden 650s merely 'Best in Class'.

BSA men would claim that it was Turner as automotive chief who stopped any further Gold Star development after 1956. And for 1958 the Delta Head T110 had achieved the reliability which was the bottom line for Thruxton and similar races, with a young Mike Hailwood and team-mate Dan Shorey winning overall. It was another good argument for a production supersports 650, along with American victories in the US TT races and in the Big Bear Run desert enduro. (In 1958, Triumphs not only won, but took eight out of the first 10 places.) Desert racing was another arena where, as top tuner Pat Owens put it, 'mostly it's reliability'. That was Henry Vale and the Comp Shop's ultimate aim also.

Reliability was not a word associated with Triumph twins from the late 1960s on. This was due to a combination of output pushed to the limit, declining production and quality control standards, and then disgusted judgements passed on amateur-fettled fifth-hand or tenth-hand machines, judgements often made in the light of more sophisticated Oriental competition. But to win a race you need to finish, and all those racing men could not have been wrong. As Gene Romero put it, 'for many years, when you rolled up to the starting line aboard a Triumph, you were considered a genuine threat.' Even Bert Hopwood, in many ways Turner's rival as well as his sometime collaborator, concluded that the Triumph twin engine was 'sound and reliable'. With one important proviso, as a Canadian dealer pointed out, Triumphs needed maintenance approximately twice as often as other British makes. If they got it, they were durable.

Edward Turner would also have known that BSAs twins which, like the Triumphs, had up until then suffered from crankshaft breakage in competition, were for 1958 adopting a stronger one-piece crank, and that the alloy-head A10 Road Rocket 650 would present a real threat, although twin carb conversions for them would be from an outside supplier only. For 1958 AMC bikes, which by then included Nortons as well as Matchless and AJS twins, although still only 600s, were offering twin carbs, as well as Royal Enfield's less-than-reliable 700 Constellation: a big Enfield with Bob MacIntyre

up had been the main challenge at Thruxton. So, although John Nelson considered that in an ideal world Turner would have held off, so that the charisma of a twin carb model would have helpfully coincided with the move to unit construction for the 650s, which he was already contemplating, events nudged him into it sooner.

Another slant on the T120's inception was provided by the late Neale Shilton in his autobiography *A Million Miles Ago*. Shilton was a fine rider and an energetic salesman for Triumph's police motorcycles like the 650 Saint, which he also helped to concoct. But every colleague of his I have talked to has agreed that this talented raconteur was also a line-shooter and the opposite of a reliable witness. On his own account, then, Shilton wrote that in the spring of 1958, it had been he who suggested to Turner that 'a Triumph named Bonneville would be a natural outcome of the Utah record', a bike with 'a more sporting appearance and a twin carburettor motor', as well as 'a two-colour finish of Utah sky blue and Salt Flats white'. The latter may be poetic hindsight, as Turner had already initiated two-tone colour schemes for 1957, part of his 'scooterisation' drive, as two colours had worked as well for Lambretta as they did for some of Britain's ageing car designs; and blue was already associated with Coventry and by extension, Triumph, who rendered the printed version of their logo in this colour.

Shilton wrote that, as anticipated, Turner objected, saying 'he did not like twin carbs, they were a difficult problem for an aircleaner'. Shilton countered that on not one of his own new, 50,000 mile-a-year twins, had he fitted an aircleaner. He added that the Yanks would only throw them away anyway 'to get more power'. This is an instance of two-peoples-divided-by-a-common-language, as in fact the inadequacy of standard British aircleaners was an on-going source of frustration to the US dirt and desert riders and racers who made up a significant part of Triumph's parish. According to one desert champion quoted in Lindsay Brooke's excellent book *Triumph Racing Motorcycles in America*, they tried everything – including Brillo pads! – before aftermarket K and M, and later

The birth of a legend. The first Bonneville for 1959 was flamboyant but shapely – and quick.

The 'name game'. Bonneville Salt Flats, Utah, where Johnny Allen's 1956 record-breaking streamliner gave the T120 its moniker.

Filtron, aircleaners were evolved.

In late August 1958, Experimental chief Frank Baker arranged an official viewing of the spivved-up twin carb T110 for ET and his senior staff. Also present were the Americans, Dennis MacCormack from TriCor plus Bill Johnson and Wilbur Ceder from JoMo, all no doubt pushing for a green light on the project. Turner, wrote Nelson, was at his most theatrical, lecturing his staff on the possibly disastrous consequences of such a high output machine, and observing in a loud stage-whisper to Frank Baker, 'My boy, this will lead us straight to Carey Street!' (Carey Street being London's bankruptcy court.)

It was already too late for the T120 to be included in either the catalogue for the following model year, or the Triumph display at the Earl's Court Show. The 1958 Show was eagerly awaited, as with the Suez Crisis and its consequences receding, enthusiasm for motorcycling had never been higher, and there had been no Show the previous year. It is not clear exactly when Turner gave his new flagship the go-ahead, but on 4 September production

commenced, and early in the month he authorised what Shilton describes as an unusual move to launch the model – which on Shilton's account was nearly disastrous. Technical journalists were invited to join Triumph staff including Shilton and Turner himself, for a long weekend in the Welsh hills, test-riding the 1959 range, including the new model. Unfortunately, on the first day one of the writers, Barry Ryerson, while riding the T120 missed a change from third gear to top, put the revs way over the red line and bent a valve-stem. He kept quiet about it, and even more unfortunately, next morning Turner was first up on the twin carb 650. When it refused to start, and then ran on one cylinder only, he became incensed and threatened to put the project on hold, which he would have been quite capable of doing. But soon, as Shilton put it, 'his engineer's instincts prevailed', and production of the T120 went ahead – although with stronger valve springs.

The Bonneville was a sensation at Earl's Court. On a 100ft (30m) show stand designed by Turner himself, under 140 neon tubes, a

Polished cases, rocker boxes and carb bell-mouths – the
first Bonnie shone.

cutaway of the new 46bhp twin carb engine
(the T110 claimed 42) was continuously
thronged by an impenetrable crush of
enthusiastic spectators. Triumph had already
proudly publicised Johnny Allen's achievement
on the Salt Flats with 'World Motorcycle Record
Holder' transfers on many models, and now the
Bonneville name hammered the point home.
Turner was often lucky, and never more so than
at that moment, for thanks largely to a pre-
election loosening of HP restrictions, the
Bonnie's launch for 1959 coincided with the
UK's last great surge in sales of new
motorcycles.

That was a bonus, starting with a bang,
which helped ensure that the Bonneville would
be a legend on both sides of the Atlantic. *The
Motor Cycle*'s 1958 Show issue might
speculate, 'are these the first motorway
models?' – motorways then being the
buzzword in Britain with the first section of the
M1 to be opened the following year, although
anyone who has ridden a 360° parallel twin
without rubber engine mounts at high speeds
for long distances will know that this line of
speculation was a dead end. But *The Motor
Cycle* had prefaced that remark with a
reference to 'the claims of the United States
market', of which Triumph was well aware. As the
Guggenheim book put it, 'the name Bonneville
was intended to play into the bike's decidedly
American orientation – and it succeeded'.

Birth pangs: 1959

In some ways, the first T120 was an uncompromising sportster – no air cleaners, no panelling, no Slickshift (a less than popular Turner automatic clutch innovation), but optional wide or close-ratio gearbox internals. Yet, possibly because of the very late decision to go ahead with the model, these first T120s appeared with the headlamp nacelle in place (which did not look good with the higher handlebars specified on US models), a touring twin-level dual seat, ungaitered forks, and for the UK even, unlike the test-bed model, touring handlebars as well as fully valenced mudguards. The latter not only looked wrong, they were wrong, regularly splitting from the sports engine's vibration. These bikes were very much adapted T110s, with some early examples retaining the 'T110' designation on Triumph's unique little triangular patent plate on the timing cover, and the cylinder head bearing the T110's casting number as well as unmachined remains of the previous inlet tract. It was still a shapely model, no question, with the elegant, Romanesque lines of its toolbox, oil tank and curvaceous petrol tank, and glittering polished cases picking up the chromed bellmouths on the twin carbs, but as Tim Remus put it, 'the first Bonneville came to the beach party in a tuxedo when everybody expected a T-shirt and jeans'. This was doubly frustrating for Americans, as the kind of stripped-down model they wanted already existed, in the shape of the single carb TR6 Trophy.

The **1959** model's most prominent *faux pas* was the initial colour scheme. Turner, with his artistic side, personally presided over the selection of his bikes' colour combinations, and while Triumph shades were usually the most attractive of all the British makes, in the past there had already been the odd error of judgement,

like the first 6T's dull greyish Thunderbird Blue. To these must be added the T120's Pearl Grey and Tangerine, the gold-lined two-tone finish divided on the tank by a chrome strip. It may be that Turner was looking sideways at another '58 Show sensation from within the BSA Group, Ariel's panelled 250 Leader with a not-dissimilar Cherokee Red and Battleship Grey colour option. Whatever the reason, the cumulative results in America were near-disastrous. For 1960 only, US Bonneville models, although their engine codes remained T120, were

Early touring-type mudguards, with front number plate surround, on the '59 T120, plus spindly forks and marginal front brake.

The 'Tangerine Dream' colour scheme took no prisoners.

redesignated (confusingly in the light of later 750 models) TR7B (low exhaust) and TR7A (high pipe) – just to dissociate themselves from the touring-styled 'Tangerine Dream' T120s, many of which stayed unsold. (Paradoxically, due to rarity and oddity value, these unique machines are now much prized. One very prominent and much photographed example actually had to be reconstructed from a T110!)

However, Meriden did not ignore this unpopularity. By mid-season, an alternative scheme, with Pearl Grey upper and gold-lined Royal Blue lower colours was offered, although according to Gerard Kane's painstaking book, *Original Triumph Bonneville*, this was only in the UK. This classic Bonnie combination, with the blue named Azure for the States, but according to Hughie Hancox, the same colour, reached there the following year. There were also other

mid-season cosmetic changes: the dual seat with white piping went to a narrower sports type as fitted on the Trophy, some plain black and some black with grey trim around their lower edges. The UK handlebars also changed from Triumph's characteristic pull-backs with their then unique 1in diameter, to a straighter type.

The UK and US models differed in detail from the start, and a further complicating factor was additional differences between the East and West Coast specifications on both Bonneville Roadsters and sports variants, which became more stringently dictated, complicating life at Meriden, as the US market grew dominant. The 1959 UK model had a 4-gallon tank with screw-on kneegrips, against the US model's 3 (Imp) gallon one, and like the Trophy, with knee grips pressed on to a mounting panel. UK machines

The polished cases of the 1959 Bonnie's engine concealed a one-piece crankshaft and hot cams.

fitted 5-pint oil tanks against the US 4-pint tanks which were Pearl grey, as opposed to the early UK model's black oil tank and tool box. During the year an 8-pint oil tank was offered as an option in America, although as John Nelson put it, 'this was not done by Meriden. TriCor and Johnsons were a law unto themselves. Many things were marketed by Pete Colman, but given Triumph parts numbers.' The '59 UK Bonnie was catalogued at 404lb (183kg) dry, which would drop to 393lb (178kg) the following year with the adoption of some American fittings. It was still a very respectable figure: BSA's A10 Road Rocket/Super Rocket weighed in at 418lb (190kg). Turner and Triumph's design philosophy had always been to 'use the minimum of metal for the maximum of work'. As Brian Jones, another Triumph designer put

it, 'at Meriden, motorcycles were drawn with a sharp pencil'. This lightness in conjunction with such a responsive engine played a large part in the Bonnie's liveliness.

No new model was going to be without its problems, and the '59 T120 was no exception. The one-piece crankshaft gained new flywheel bolts mid-season after some earlier trouble with breakage. With the alloy head, in US competition the 8.5:1 pistons crowns could collapse and their skirts distort, so the crowns were progressively thickened and the skirts given increased clearance from the crankshaft bobweights. The clutch also still suffered under hard use, and mid-year, the hardening treatment for the clutch centre was improved. In the same way in mid-season the gearbox camplate periphery became induction hardened.

Finally there were the twin carbs, with their

float bowls 'chopped' and a single remote float chamber rubber-mounted behind them from a block fastened to the frame's upright tube. In competition conditions, this set-up gave a definite advantage, with a 1961 *Motor Cycle* road test finding that with it, available rpm rose from 6,800 to 7,500, and top speed from around 110 to 117mph (177–188kph). But in regular use, the remote chamber was troublesome, being prone to fuel surge, which caused high speed misfiring, as well as fussy running at low revs. Mid-season the chamber was moved forward to a position between the carburettors, but this was an interim solution.

The Bonneville's mechanicals however were not its fundamental problems. These remained its brakes and handling. The 7in rear brake was respectable but the 8in sls front, despite an alteration to the angle of the front brake cam lever for improved leverage, remained marginal in view of the bike's thundering performance. The same was true of the T110 chassis, with its spindly forks liable to get skittish and wash out under hard acceleration, and its unbraced swinging arm still prone to induce high-speed weave and wobble. As already stated, this could be learned and managed, but was scarcely reassuring; although some relished it as part of the Bonnie's 'flair and fire'. Meriden, however, decided to do something about it.

1960: chrysalis to butterfly

The **1960** T120 was definitely a different-looking machine to its predecessor. The nacelle was gone, replaced by a chromed separate headlamp shell which permitted the previously optional rev counter to be fitted as standard to American models, except on the high-pipe off-road TR7A. The twinned instruments were a real Bonnie feature, although they would not become standard on UK models until 1965.

Mudguards changed to an alloy blade at the front with the front number plate no longer featuring a chromed surround, and an unvalenced steel job at the rear. The forks were claimed to have gained two-way damping. They were certainly redesigned to reduce spring friction, and they contained more damping oil. They adopted a new crown and combined fork shrouds/headlamp brackets, with glossy black gaiters.

With a better-padded black seat with white piping, plus the blue and grey colour scheme, the Bonnie had emerged. The jutting chrome headlamp topping a steeper fork, the rakish angle of the flatter handlebars, the inward curves of the tank, the chromed badges which hugged it and the knee grips, the splayed exhausts and protruding twin carbs, the lightness of the new guards and the open-sided rear lamp support (a Turner innovation which doubled as a lifting handle) – all created a symphony in metal that was highly suggestive of speed. Truly this was the bike that 'looked as if it was doing 100mph when it was standing still'.

The frame, while still of brazed-lug construction and still featuring single top- and seat-tubes, now featured twin front downtubes. With a head-angle steepened from 64.5 to 67° to tighten the steering, in conjunction with an all-new rear frame, now attached at the bottom by a substantial lug at the base of the seat-tube, the new chassis with its shorter wheelbase was a distinct improvement on the road, despite the swinging arm remaining unbraced. Steering was marginally heavier but conversely there was less front end lightness at speed, and the bike was still highly manoeuvrable. An additional bonus was that the new frame damped down vibration for a smoother ride. In conjunction with the flatter bars, the riding position became a markedly jockey-like crouch. One aspect not mentioned in contemporary road tests was the T120's relative lack of ground clearance. While their lowness made the bikes ideal for town riding, it did mean that their undercarriage was near the deck, and over-enthusiastic cornering could rapidly lead to finding yourself running wide round a left-hander in a shower of sparks – although rockers would relish this as an outward and visible sign that someone was really trying. Other than that, the new frame did however contain a serious flaw of its own.

The electrics were also revised. The ignition remained by magneto, although now fitted with automatic advance/retard as standard, and the K2FC competition mag now standard for American models. The dynamo was gone, replaced, behind a new primary chaincase with a telltale bulge, by a Lucas RM15 alternator. Because the new headlamp featured qd connections to favour conversion for sports, the headlamp switch moved to an inconvenient position below the right side of the dual seat nose, facing outwards. The qd headlamps were a mixed blessing, sometimes spontaneously disconnecting and plunging the night rider into darkness. In fact, these headlamps were only the tip of an iceberg of unsatisfactory electrics. Brooke and Gaylin quote one Detroit dealer as

The chaincase bulge indicated an alternator for the lights
from 1960 on, with magneto behind the cylinder for ignition.

declaring that 'the 1960 electrics were beyond bad', going on to instance the lack of voltage control, batteries split by vibration, ineffectual dip-switches, and poor quality wiring harnesses. At the 1961 Triumph US dealer convention, the Lucas rep was roundly booed!

On the other side of the crankcase, machines fitted with rev counters had timing covers incorporating the tacho drive take-off, as these were now gear-driven from the exhaust camshaft pinion retaining nut; on machines so equipped, the triangular patent plate was relocated on the bulge this created. The revised primary chaincase meant a new exhaust pipe with a different bend on that side. At the other end of it, the silencers acquired a detachable mute. Late on in the model year, the twin carburettors lost the remote float chamber

and became the standard 1⅟₁₆in Monobloc instruments, a change some owners had already made for themselves, and one which gave smoother running at low revs. With the change to normal left and right-handed instruments, according to Hughie Hancox, the previous plethora of tubes with clips around them was changed to pre-made transparent pipes.

Traditionally, American riders first checked the standing quarter mile time on a model, where British ones looked at the top speed. This may help explain why the 1960 Bonneville's gearing was lowered overall, with the previous 24-tooth engine sprocket replaced by one with 22 teeth, and the rear sprocket dropping from 46 to 43 teeth. A new gearbox plunger spring was also fitted.

The oil tank internals and mountings were

revised, and with the new frame, a new petrol tank was fitted, which although of similar appearance, was now with three-point fixing, as well as being rubber-mounted at three points, and like a Wideline Featherbed Norton's, retained by a rubber-lined chrome strap running from front to rear. Unfortunately, this new tank may have contributed to problems with the new frame. With the latter lacking a tank rail, the front of the tank was now fixed directly to the frame's twin downtubes. In US off-road competition there were some instances of the downtubes fracturing immediately below the steering head lug. In December's Big Bear Run, Edward Turner personally witnessed a tragic example of this, where the rider was killed. He immediately initiated a test programme at MIRA to identify the problem, and from engine/frame No D1563 the frame was redesigned to incorporate an extra, lower, tank rail running horizontally from the top of the downtubes to a point on the top tube beneath the rear tank mounting.

The rev counter was a must-have Bonnie optional extra; the drive required a special timing cover.

1961 and 1962: pre-unit flare and fade

The revised frame cured the problem, but had a nasty side effect. It increased vibration again, not so much for the rider as for the bicycle, with a rash of breakages for the tank's chrome retaining strap, which for **1961** was altered to stainless steel. The lower tank rail also made the engine harder to work on at the top end, and to get out of the frame. The '61 Bonnie however was and remains a highly desirable machine. The colour scheme was revised, now with a different lighter Sky Blue as the upper rather than the lower colour on the tank, with gold-lined Silver below, more like what Shilton said he had originally envisaged, and a definitive look for the Bonneville. The petrol tank itself was strengthened at its nose to counter vibration, and became a catalogued 3 gallons as standard – although when measured by *The Motor Cycle* on a TR6 on test, one example actually held 3½ gallons. The oil tank, silver in the '61 colour scheme, gained anti-vibration

The 1961 tank retaining strap was made of stainless steel.

mountings, which were also adopted mid-year for the toolbox.

The steering head angle was revised again, now being 2° less steep at 65°, which was better suited to American off-road riding, although desert riders would often modify their (usually single carb) twins by a further 4° or 5°. The T120s front fork now fitted an aluminium damper sleeve between the bushes within each leg.

Attention was also paid to the gearbox. Overall gearing was lowered a little further by the use of a 21-tooth engine sprocket. Like the steering head revision and the smaller tank, the lower gearing was silent witness to increasing US market domination. By 1962, with the pre-election HP concessions having been rapidly reversed once Harold Macmillan had got in again, the UK market for new motorcycles had fallen by a stunning 50 per cent against its

1959–60 peak. It was not just the HP, but a phenomenon observed previously in Germany. Up to a certain point (1959 in the case of the UK), a continuous rise in real wages had increased demand for both motorcycles and cars as primary transport. After that point the demand would be for cars only. From then on, it was down to young rebels and America.

In the gearbox itself, Torrington needle roller bearings supplanted the previous plain bushes for the layshaft. A larger thrust washer bearing at each end of the layshaft was also fitted, with the main casing and inner cover suitably modified. Primary chain tension had always been adjusted by moving the separate box, and now an additional (and inaccessible) adjuster screw was fitted inboard of the box's top clamp, to improve alignment.

Further American-orientated measures

A coiled spring. The 1961 Bonnie's explosive acceleration
was implicit in its taut looks.

included a folding kick-start as standard, and a
4.00 x 18in rear tyre replacing the previous 3.50
x 18in. In the engine, to counter ringing, the
cylinder head had its outer fins linked by
vertical buttresses, and internally a greater
thickness of aluminium around the exhaust
valve insert to try to counter the eight-stud
head's tendency to crack. Most significantly of
all, the brakes were improved, with the friction
strips resited at the trailing end of the shoes
and the shoes themselves made fully floating.
Although the brakes were still not truly
adequate to the performance, these measures
made the 8in front one in particular one of the
best among its contemporaries.

Riders loved the '61 Bonnie. A contemporary
Motor Cycling test deployed the phrases
'explosive acceleration', 'abundant vitality', and
'extraordinary vigour and tractability', the latter

attribute being emphasised when they wrote
that 'in London traffic it was one of the most
pleasant machines we have ever used', this
user friendliness always being such a key to
the T120's appeal. They were also honest
enough to note that 'on really fast corners the
machine was not completely steady; there was
a certain amount of rear wheel movement'. *The
Motor Cycle* also liked the T120 they tested,
with its light, strong clutch, 'superb' brakes and
exciting performance, although they found the
suspension hard and the twin carbs difficult to
synchronise satisfactorily.

Twenty years later in *Classic Bike*, editor Mike
Nicks found a '61 Bonnie 'almost ridiculously
easy to ride' compared with contemporary
multis and with tuned singles. He loved the
looks and considered that the duplex frame had
largely eliminated the hinged-in-the-middle

The classic Classic. The '61 Bonnie was the peak for the rocker era.

feeling. He found his test bike handled reliably 'under brisk but reasonable cornering demands', and that its compact size and good ground clearance made its manoeuvrability exceptional in bank-to-bank terms. The brakes were OK at low speeds but the 8in front degenerated into mushiness under hard application, although the 7in rear could be locked up. With a crank balanced by specialist Alan Dudley Ward, vibration from the engine only became serious after 4,000rpm, and at 6,500rpm 'the entire bike was jangling furiously'. His overall judgement after riding the '61 was that the Bonneville was the best parallel twin.

The **1962** T120 was largely similar to its predecessor, as the factory got ready for the change to a unit format. Its engine, however, was further modified with US needs in mind.

The crankshaft fitted a wider, heavier flywheel for even more scrambler-like low-down grunt, although the throttle response became a little slower. The crankshaft balance factor was increased from 50 to 71 per cent, and then from engine/frame No D17043, to an 85 per cent factor, as the previous crankshaft with its straight-sided balance weight cheeks was replaced by one with pear-shaped webs. This produced some improvement with vibration, which as we have seen had been having troublesome effects over the previous year. The camshaft drive pinions with three-keyways, previously optional, now became standard.

For the UK the colour scheme remained the same, although the oil tanks and toolboxes were now black rather than silver. For the US models it was Flame, a metallic scarlet for the

The Sky Blue and Silver Sheen colours for 1961 were some of the best ever.

upper tank, and gold-lined Silver Sheen for the lower, with models early in the year having Silver Sheen oil tanks and toolboxes, and only later standardising on black. The seat became two-tone, with a grey lower trim strip, black sides, white piping and a grey top.

The petrol pipes were rearranged so that both carburettors could be fed from one tap, by a connecting pipe between the float chambers giving a reserve for the first time, although hard riders soon found that it was advisable to keep both taps open at high speed for best results. The rear suspension units, already firm, were stiffened still further by the use of 145lb/in springs. Third gear was raised slightly. The alternator became the Lucas RM19 type, although for the Bonneville, still with a low output stator to help guard against overcharging,

always a danger as long as the 'switch-controlled – to balance generator output' system was still in place. A new rectifier was also fitted.

The end of the 1962 season brought the end of the pre-unit Triumphs (the 500s had been unitised by 1960), and as John Nelson wrote, 'so much changed from the original established design that many said that the character of the first Bonneville was now lost for ever', although as Mike Clay points out in his book *Café Racers*, plenty of rockers were still prepared to sell their soul on the HP to own a new one. But Clay confirmed that 'café racers everywhere hated the '63 unit-engined Bonnies', which were felt to have lost much of their charisma. The pre-unit engines, as well as remaining the rockers' choice, whether in stock, tweaked or Tritonized form, have

The works

The pre-unit T120 Bonneville's engine was in a direct line with Turner's original Speed Twin. Like the latter, it was a parallel twin cylinder motor with a separate, four-speed gearbox. It featured twin camshafts set fore and aft of its iron cylinder block, and driven by gears. Where the T120 differed significantly was in its cylinder head, which unlike those of the iron-engined Speed Twin and Thunderbird, was alloy – and featured what was to be the Bonnie's trademark, twin carburettors.

The engine was based on a vertically split cast aluminium crankcase. This carried the crankshaft on two heavy-duty ball race main bearings, with an additional ball race having been added to the timing side for 1954 to create the so-called 'big bearing' motor. The crankshaft itself had originally been a three-piece, bolted-up item, but on the 650s for the Bonnie's first model year, this changed significantly to a one-piece forging, with 1⅜in diameter journals. Threaded over the outer crank cheek was the central cast iron flywheel, which was then pressed into place and centrally located by three ⅞in radial bolts. These bolts passed through the outer periphery of the flywheel into threaded holes in the crankshaft itself. The crankshaft balance factor for the first T120s was 50 per cent.

The 360° crankshaft meant that the solid skirt pistons rose and fell together, which helped eliminate carburation bias problems, although it did create fundamental primary vibration. Since 1955, con rods had been of H-section alloy, with shell big-end bearings. The T120's pistons gave a compression ratio of 8.5:1. The alloy cylinder head, with its characteristic splayed exhaust ports blending into the graceful bends of the pipes, was derived from the Delta head, so called due to its bifurcated shape, as well as the name of the firm that cast it, which had been introduced on the Bonnie's direct antecedent, the T110. One criticism of Turner's design with its fore-and-aft pushrod tubes had been that the front tube to some extent impeded the flow of cooling air, and meant that Triumphs ran hot. Early iron-head versions of the 650 T110 had been particularly prone to overheating, and

reportedly to subsequent distortion and warping of the cylinder head although John Nelson says that the real problem was not distortion but the iron head's failure to lose heat as petrol octane ratings, and consequently compression ratios rose, which led to holed pistons, especially in export models. So for 1956, the 650 had come equipped with a new, die-cast, light-alloy cylinder head, with cast-in air passages. This head had also eliminated previous external oil pipes, as it drained oil directly into the pushrod cover tubes.

The Delta head was adapted for the Bonneville to take two splayed 1 1/16in Amal Monobloc carburettors, served by an Amal GP central rubber-mounted remote-float bowl. The head itself was still retained by eight fixing bolts and remained prone to cracking between the valve-seats and the inboard stud holes. The Delta's two separate alloy rocker boxes had been redesigned, and within each of them, two rockers were mounted on a common spindle, with thrust washers and coil spring washers to help reduce noise and wear. Each rocker had a ball end

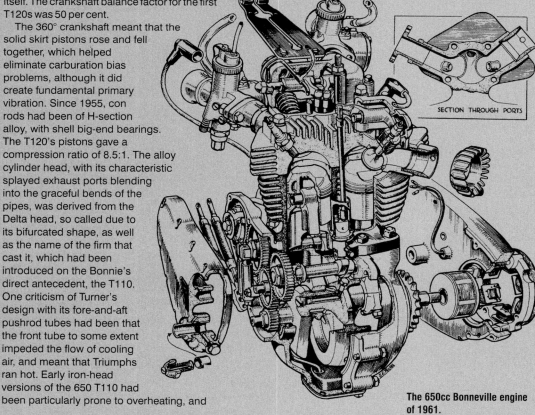

SECTION THROUGH PORTS

The 650cc Bonneville engine of 1961.

on its inner arm, and on its outer end, an adjuster with a lock nut. Access for adjustment was via four screw caps, which were famously prone to unscrew themselves and fall off.

The valve inserts were cast-in, and the valves in their cast-iron guides were set at 90° to one another, and controlled by dual coil valve springs. The valves were operated by alloy pushrods located in their tubes in pairs between the bores, in turn worked by the two high-mounted, gear-driven camshafts. Precise valve timing, using the optional camshaft pinions with their three alternative keyways, was one way of reaching top performance. For the first T120, the cams featured the legendary E3134 profile for the inlet and E3325 for the exhaust, the former being based on the American-developed 'Q' sports cam.

Lubrication was effected by Triumph's vertically-mounted, dual plunger oil pump. This was driven by an off-centre pin incorporated into the timing side (ie right) end of the nut – which retained the inlet camshaft. The pump fed oil, ideally at 50-60psi, to the big end bearings via a bush in the timing cover and drillings in the crankshaft. Oil feed was controlled by an oil pressure relief valve and a button indicator which protruded from the right side of the polished, shapely timing cover when the pressure was correct, so the rider could check it with his foot. In the dry sump system, all the oil eventually drained to the bottom of the crankcase, and the mesh filter located there, mounted on a sump plate with four bolts. Oil was scavenged from there via a pipe and returned to the 5-pint oil tank.

Primary drive was via a single-strand chain. The four-spring clutch, which incorporated the transmission shock absorber, ran wet and featured five corked driving and six steel driven plates. It was mounted on the mainshaft of the sturdy four-speed gearbox. This was conventionally British, with the layshaft mounted below the mainshaft, and the output sprocket mounted on a sleeve gear. Top (fourth) gear was a direct 1:1 ratio, and the three others involved two pairs of gears on the main and lay shafts. The two gear selectors were mounted on a rod positioned in front of the gearshaft. They were shifted by a flat circular camplate, pivoted on the front face of the gear casing and located by a spring-loaded plunger. This plunger was geared to a quadrant pivoted on a pin, and moved one gear at a time by a positive-stop mechanism.

Ignition for the T120 was by the tried-and-tested Lucas 6-volt magneto which sports riders still demanded, both the standard K2F with manual advance or, on some US machines, the K2FC Red label competition variant. The magneto was mounted to the rear of the cylinder. Other electrical functions were still undertaken by a forward mounted Lucas E3L dynamo, prior to the 1960 model year when the alternator took over.

emerged as the classic Classics in the Bonneville story. This is partly from rarity value, as less were built, and partly from recognition of what can only be called class, which they exuded from every line. They also, as we shall discuss in the next chapter, could provide a fundamentally sweeter ride.

The beautiful '61 model in our photos was brought to the studio by Tony Mortimer on behalf of its owner Roger Anderson. A seasoned rider who ran a Vincent 1000 twin in the rocker era and today restores Velocettes, Tony was still knocked back by the '61 Bonnie's acceleration – 'When you get going – phew!' But despite that year's reputation for increased vibration, he found the bike quite smooth at 60mph.

No six-footer, Tony found the 'jockey-like' riding position comfortable, and the centre stand beautifully easy to use, in combination with the curved lifting handles whose line gracefully echoed that of the rear mudguard. He was not, however, impressed with the model's brakes, despite the adoption of fully floating shoes for that year: 'a 100mph machine with the brake of a Bantam', he called it. Both the Vincent's dual front brakes and his Velocette Thruxton's 7½in front stopper had proved to him that drum brake designs could be a lot more effective, but the Bonnie would have to wait another seven years before it would get the front brake it deserved. Otherwise, overwhelming impressions were favourable.

Roger Anderson the owner was also very happy with his Bonnie. He had paid £6,250 for the '61, some £3,000 more than a top Sixties unit T120 would have set him back. Like Tony, Roger was also an active Velocette rider, so why had he splurged on that particular Bonneville?

'I'm 52. The Bonnie, along with the Gold Star, was *the* icon when I was young.' Was he specifically a pre-unit fan? 'I had a 1977 T140 Jubilee 750 Bonneville, and in some ways it was a nicer bike from A to B, but it wasn't as much fun as the T120 – this one is very raw. I have also got a 1939 Speed Twin, which is equally good in its way. Of all the Triumphs, those two are the ones.'

The unbearable lightness of Bonnie:
1963–70 Unit T120s

The shift to unit construction for Triumph's flagship may not have suited the purists or those thoroughly accustomed to its pre-unit predecessors, but with increased American demand in mind, as Edward Turner might have said, it suited the occasion. Unit engines were cheaper to produce than those with a separate box, and the change provided a natural point to abandon the popular but obsolescent and expensive magneto in favour of coil ignition. The resulting machine was compact, and even lighter than before (at a striking 363lb/165kg dry). And, thanks to Doug Hele, it handled.

In 1961 Edward Turner had persuaded Bert Hopwood, then the Managing Director of Norton, to join him at Meriden, as the failing fortunes of the AMC Group, which owned Norton, began to suck the Bracebridge Street firm down. Turner was now in his early 60s and cited ill-health (he was a diabetic) to persuade Hopwood that the latter would soon have some real control; although under the BSA Group's new Chairman, the confusingly named Eric Turner, this was not to be. The following year, two other Norton men, Brian Jones and Doug Hele, a long-time collaborator with Hopwood, also came to Triumph from Norton. Hele took the title of Development Engineer.

They brought with them the accumulated engineering knowledge necessary to progressively transform the Triumph twins into machines which could take on the Nortons and distinguish themselves on road and track. In UK production racing, after three years of Norton victory, Triumphs began a winning

streak at the key Thruxton 500 endurance event. As the distinguished journalist and technical writer Vic Willoughby put it, Doug Hele's enormous experience 'vastly improved the steering and broadened the power band' of the 650 twins. The latter point, with concentration on the realistically more useful mid-range rather than on ultimate top end, helped ensure that the Bonnie maintained its proverbially user-friendly character, even if that policy would take a dent for a couple of years in the middle of the decade. John Nelson wrote that around 1966 'there was a heart-felt feeling growing amongst many at Meriden that the amount and type of horsepower being built into the standard over-the-counter Bonnie was more than enough, and had transformed it from a high-speed tourer into nothing short of a production racer in disguise'. But progressive changes would restore the Bonnie's character as a great all-rounder for the best years of all, from 1968 to 1970.

It is 1963, and 650 Triumphs now handled – or they would
do when the front fork was changed …

1963: first unit

Like the first T120 itself in 1959, the earliest unit-construction Bonneville in **1963** was something of a hybrid model, sharing a good deal of its cycle parts with its predecessor. However, in one significant area it represented a return to 1959 itself, as after the duplex frame years, Hele's redesigned chassis now featured a typically Triumph single front downtube.

The new frame had a downtube significantly thicker (1⅝in diameter, 12 gauge) than previous examples, while retaining the previous 65° steering head angle. And at the rear, a brazed-in forged lug carried a new swinging-arm pivot. This lug had each of its ends secured to the rear engine mounting plates, and the plates in turn were bolted to struts on the rear sub-frame. The swinging arm itself was also

stiffened up. The result was an immediate, unmissable gain in handling.

'Road-holding on my 1963 Bonnie is miles better than that of my 1962 duplex-framed Trophy', a young enthusiast wrote in to *Motor Cycle*'s 1965 Reader's Report on the model. Doug Hele with his questing nature was less satisfied and, as Vic Willoughby reported in November 1962 on a pre-production unit prototype, which was held above the ton for miles at MIRA and on the M1, 'occasionally at 100mph upwards I found a trace of the old weaving… (Hele's) chief aim now is to keep the front wheel glued to the deck, for it is only then

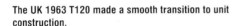

The UK 1963 T120 made a smooth transition to unit construction.

A compact motor, with engine and gearbox still clearly defined.

that the castor action due to fork trail can exert its stabilising effect on steering.' But effective action on that would have to wait until the new front end came in for 1964, as for 1963 the Bonnie still wore the former spindly 'inside spring' forks, although with a new top yoke.

The new engine layout contained several changes within its reassuringly familiar-looking format, with the shape of the gearbox and of the triangular timing chest still clearly discernible. The triangular patent plate was restored to a central position, with the rev counter still driven from the exhaust camshaft,

but now from the front of the primary drive side of the crankcase. The oil-pressure indicator was also moved from the outer face to the front edge of the timing cover. The engine and gearbox retained separate supplies of lubricant, and on a practical level, the gearbox could still be serviced independently of the engine.

The compact, sculptural motor's uncluttered look was in large part due to the elimination of the magneto for ignition purposes. The primary chaincase had been styled with a shapely flute, a horizontal coma embossed with the Triumph

logo. The chaincase no longer supported the left footrest; for that year only, both rests bolted directly on to frame lugs positioned just below them. The new crankcases were both lighter and stiffer than their predecessors, a significant contribution to the Bonnie's overall low weight.

Along with lighting, ignition was now taken care of by the 6-volt Lucas RM19 alternator, with coil ignition via twin MA6 coils. Twin Lucas 4CA contact breakers, also driven by the exhaust camshaft, were neatly located behind a chromed, circular plate in the timing cover. Both light and ignition switches were relocated in the left-hand side panel. Unfortunately this electrical system would constitute one of the new Bonnie's big let-downs. Since late in the previous year at D18149, the potentially dangerous detachable headlamp arrangement, however, had been dropped.

At the top end, a new cylinder head with nine-stud fixing effectively addressed the previous problem of cracking heads, and was often retro-fitted to pre-unit machines. The ninth, centre, stud was inaccessible, but did help gas sealing between the cylinders. The rocker boxes were now unpolished, and featured stylish horizontal finning, and there was increased finning also on the alloy head itself. The cross-slotted inspection caps were slightly shallower than previously and now came with milled edges and spring steel clips to bear down on these, but that did not cure the caps' tendency to unscrew and fly off down the road. The alloy inlet manifolds now featured steel screw-in adapters.

Internally the crankshaft, although still with an 85 per cent balance factor, had been revised and lightened, with the flywheel retaining bolts now fastened by Loctite rather than relying on shake-proof washers. The new, stiffer shaft featured an extended right side journal with a ground surface, in place of the previous timing cover oil control bush; it now engaged with a new oil seal in the cover, which was beneficial for constant oil pressure to the big ends. The oil pump had its scavenge plunger relocated on the left. The new crankshaft, however, did initially carry a downside, in that its stiffness could pressure the main bearings diametrically and this caused some instances of mains failure.

The transmission was also revised, the most prominent feature being the new ⅜in duplex primary chain, replacing the previous single strand item, and tensioned by an awkward-to-operate rubber-faced blade. There was also a new three-spring clutch with an extra pair of plates and a revised centre, as well as a three-vane shock-absorber. The clutch operating mechanism worked by three ⅜in ball bearings in a ramp between a pair of steel pressings, one secured to the gearbox cover and the other rotated by operation of the clutch cable. As the pressing rotated, the balls rode up beside the seating and imparted a lateral thrust to the clutch pushrod. In good fettle, this arrangement could give a smoother change than most separate gearboxes, but for that everything had to be in top condition, and the components were not nearly as robust as their predecessors.

There were detailed changes to the cycle parts which both streamlined production, and for economies of scale dovetailed with the other unit twins, both Triumph and BSA. The wheels for UK models became 18in all round (3.25 x 18in front, 3.50 x 18in rear), while the US machines retained their previous sizes (3.25 x 19in front, 4.00 x 18in rear). The front mudguard gained different bridge and rear stays, while the rear guard became a new blade-type, but still with a raised central stripe. The dual seat became hinged, and the petrol tank, in both sizes, although looking the same, was a new type, with recesses underneath for the twin coils, and thinner, glued-on knee grips. In another near-imperceptible break with Triumph's previously unique styling, handlebars became of conventional ⅞in diameter, although their clamps were shimmed so that the previous 1in bars could be fitted if preferred. On the bars, the handlebar grips were no longer embossed with 'Triumph'.

The new Bonnie came in a striking, if slightly puzzling finish – all Alaskan white. Did someone admire the police 'Snowdrop' twins (although their white was less of an ivory shade), or was this a sop to Honda's contemporary 'You Meet The Nicest People' publicity campaign? It seemed particularly bizarre given the stated American preference

for black bikes. The '63 T120 had a white petrol tank badged as previously, white mudguards with a gold, black-lined centre stripe, but black for the revised toolbox and oil tank, whose filler cap was now out of sight under the dual seat.

Since 1960, for the US market, the Bonneville in addition to the T120R (for Road) had also been available as the high-pipe T120C (for Competition) variants, and as mentioned, from then on the East and West Coast variants had begun to diverge. The West Coast's legally required safety strap on the dual seat was only one of the variations, which included different exhaust systems, gearing and states of tune, as well as mudguards, seats and sometimes colour schemes. These can be pieced together by use particularly of Gaylin's *Triumph*

Motorcycle Restoration Guide, Roy Bacon's *Triumph Twin Restoration*, and of course John Nelson's *Bonnie*.

What can be seen from the 1963-on variants, was that while the West Coast competition bikes favoured out-and-out off-road trim for playing in the desert, East Coast forest-bound enduro-type events meant that 500 Triumphs were the competition tool of choice, and so the East Coast 650s became early examples of the 'street scrambler' phenomenon. The 1963 East Coast T120C, although it wore a bash plate and air filters, sported a headlamp plus short silencers on its high level exhaust system, where the West Coast T120C had a straight-through exhaust and no lights at all. In line with this Californian balls-out approach, Brooke and

Gaylin's excellent book *Triumph Motorcycles in America* confirms that in competition terms, the West Coast wanted more power, where the East Coast looked for greater reliability.

Until 1968 the only AMA-recognised Grand National sport where the 650 was eligible would be US TT races. TTs were usually run on a quarter-mile kidney-shaped track of dry clay, which gave both left and right turns as opposed to the one-way only flat-tracks. And to keep things interesting, halfway around the track they added an aviating high-jump! Highly tuned versions of the West Coast T120C, with

T120C engine number prefixes, but known as TT Specials, were first supplied to JoMo and then to TriCor for 1963. They were to be a spectacularly successful and enduring part of the Bonneville legend.

Reliability was one area where both countries would be disappointed again with the 1963 machines' electrics. The problem began with the design of the 4CA contact breakers. On these, the points plates were a mounting plate for both the two sets of points which this system's twin coils required. The plates also had to accommodate two condensers. As the points were mounted on the same plate, it was not possible to time each of the two sets individually, so variations in the timing had to be compensated for, imprecisely, by varying the points gap. In addition, the inadequate 'switch-controlled' voltage regulation system was still in place, leading to boiled batteries, particularly with the 6-volt system – one Reader's Report owner needed five batteries in four years, along with three rectifiers, two alternators and no fewer than 19 headlamp-mounted ammeters; parallel twin vibrations had a habit of making the latter go open-circuit. Becoming sidelined by defective electrics is particularly frustrating for a rider – and for the Bonnie there were more troubles to come.

Aside from the still marginal brakes – several Reader's Report riders had discovered oval drums on their new Bonnevilles – the other major penalty of the change to unit construction was the somewhat harsher quality of the engine. 'Within five miles after leaving the factory,' wrote Neale Shilton, 'I was regretting the change. Vibration had arrived and smooth power transmission had gone.' Hughie Hancox in his *Tales of Triumph Motorcycles* amplified on the subject more thoughtfully. '. . . the problems with the larger [unit] twins,' he wrote, 'were all due to rigidity. The earlier pre-unit bikes did vibrate but it was liveable with due to the bikes overall flexibility. Having separate engine, gearbox and transmission, a lot more give – and indeed forgiveness – was apparent, but with the unit-construction 650 engine, and even the later 750 twins where the complete engine was a stressed member of a very rigid frame, there was no forgiveness at all.'

These views however were from men well familiar with the earlier pre-unit machines, and have to be balanced against the Guggenheim book's observation that 'at the time, vibration was embraced as part of the bikes' charm'. If this seems far-fetched, consider that even today

The '63 Bonnie's clean, classic instrument layout.

the highly successful Harley-Davidson twins, despite their Evo rubber-mounted engines, have a carefully calculated amount of vibration engineered into them to convey that macho 'real machine' flavour. Overall, the unit 650, shakes and all, passed the test of public acceptance with flying colours. 'Throughout the Sixties', wrote Tim Remus, 'the Bonneville and TR6 were the motorcycles to own. The kid on the street wanted either a Bonnie or a Harley Sportster.' Meriden's twins have been called 'a triumph of development over design', and never more so than in this key transition from pre-unit to unit power plants. As John Nelson put it to me, 'the Bonneville was a constant integrated design that incorporated changes as they happened, like Jaguar. Even if people weren't interested in bikes, they appreciated this.'

1964–7: some refinement and expanded production

In 1964 there was a change at BSA/Triumph Board level that would facilitate the Bonnie's golden age for sales. Eric Turner appointed the dynamic Harry Sturgeon, a former de Havilland aircraft executive, as both Chief Executive and Marketing Director of the motorcycle division. Sturgeon would preside over the attempted integration of BSA and Triumph as a single division, which was not always popular. Brooke and Gaylin record that in America in 1966, when it was announced that the BSA and Triumph dealers would have to sell each others' products, the forthright Texas Triumph specialist Jack Wilson of Big D, summed it up as 'a great deal for the BSA dealers … but it's like offering Triumph dealers the clap'.

Sturgeon did however put resources into Meriden which permitted their US sales to rise from 6,300 for 1963, to an official order programme of 28,700 for 1967. Of that total,

6,200 were 650s going to the West Coast, while 13,800 of the big twins went to the East. These figures emphasise the significant dependence of the factory's fortunes on the relatively short selling season in the East, which ran for just 10 weeks from April to mid-June. This dependence was quickly grasped by a workforce at Meriden which would ultimately expand to more than 2,200 to meet the demand, and by the unions representing them. Sturgeon's overriding interest in raising production and sales meant that he agreed impatiently to wage demands, and this set the mould for the 'weak management/strong union' scenario which would decisively affect the Bonnie's future.

Meanwhile, **1964** saw the T120's handling raised another notch with the arrival of the

The '64 US T120, with beefier forks.

'external spring' front forks, with their larger diameter shrouds, bigger gaiters, slightly increased damping oil, improved oil seal arrangements, and springs going round the outside of the fork inner tubes rather than inside them. These early examples were found very harsh in operation. The mudguards were modified, with the front one now steel except on some US T120C models, which had polished alloy. The front guard's centre brace was also altered, both to allow different diameter wheels and to match the new fork; the previous flat brace changed to a tubular one running parallel to the forks over the top of the wheel for increased rigidity.

In the engine, the previous year's main bearing failures meant that 'three-spot' bearings giving greater clearance were now fitted, with increased pre-loading of the bearing. They did not entirely cure drive side mains failure. The crankcase casting was revised in the sump filter area to allow a larger gauze filter, a larger drain plug, and improved scavenging. The crankcase breathing was also modified, with the breather now venting from the drive side of the inlet cam via a T-piece into the oil tank froth tower, and thence via a pipe

running along the right side of the rear mudguard to atmosphere. The oil tank itself featured revised mountings and separate drain plugs. Gearing on the US T120C models was lowered by changing the 19T gearbox sprocket to an 18T item.

The gearbox sprocket splines and high gear splines were widened along with alterations to the sprocket cover plate and its oil seal, and the kick-start lever also got a revised oil seal. Much of this represented valiant efforts to counter the Triumph's proverbial oil leaks, but as Brooke and Gaylin confirmed, these would remain a standing joke in America. Vertically split crankcases, and 'the minimum of metal' principle applied to joint faces, were the main culprits, as well as specific weak spots like the pushrod cover tube joints.

The '64 Bonnie's power was up, with the inlet valve, now of superior Nimonic material, increased to the Thruxton Bonneville's $1\frac{19}{32}$in diameter, and the exhaust to $1\frac{7}{16}$in. Factor in new Amal 389 carburettors with their chokes enlarged to $1\frac{1}{8}$in and the result was a claimed

The Bonneville's engine power was increased for 1964. Note the one-piece US air cleaners.

47bhp at 6,700rpm – although in America, puzzlingly, the T120's claimed output was 52bhp from then on. The carburettors were now handed left and right, with a flexible pipe linking their inlet stubs to help achieve steady slow running; and US models now wore a single, elongated black can-like air filter spanning both carbs, as standard, although it made the side panel-mounted switches inaccessible.

On the cycle side, the rear chainguard was enlarged, and the rear brake light switch was modified to a 'pull-on' type. The petrol tank featured a fulfilled version of the previous year's colour scheme, with Alaskan White lower, but a black-striped Gold upper. These colours were also separated in a different way, with the upper colour now following the lower edge of the tank badge and surrounding the whole knee grip. Mudguards were white with a black-lined gold stripe. A Lucas S55 cut-out switch was back on the handlebars. The footrests were now mounted on the rear engine plates, and this meant a redesigned rear brake pedal, with the brake rod on initial examples being kinked and passing to the inside of the rear frame tube. Shilton was particularly scathing about the dangerous impracticality of this arrangement, and claimed that he got the rod changed back to a straight one passing behind the left suspension unit, with replacements sent out for machines already despatched. And in a retrograde piece of 'progress', the speedo and tacho where fitted, changed from Chronometrics to the far less stable and accurate Smiths Magnetic instruments, with a grey centre circle on their faces. Not for nothing would UK police machines maintain calibrated versions of the previous Chronometric jobs, to the end.

Bob Currie tested a '64 Bonnie for *The Motor Cycle*, and focused on the combination of power and docility, calling it 'a Tarzan in city suiting … Given its head it will whistle up into treble figures … Such a model could be a real handful in city streets – lumpy, erratic, straining at the leash. But not so. [It is] a gentlemanly, unobtrusive tractable traffic threader, quite amenable to be trickled along at 30 (or less) in top…' But when you did twist the grip, soon

'the needle is much further round the dial than you had imagined it to be … mainly because the power flows in as a surging tide rather than as a noticeable kick in the pants.' Up-changes could be made at an indicated 48mph (77kph) in first, 66 (106) in second and about 90 (145) in third, but the Magnetic speedo was found to be around 10mph (16kph) optimistic. Still, a true 90mph could be held with a normal riding position on the motorway, while chinning produced a true 108mph (174kph). Currie liked the riding position despite a slightly tall seat height, with the UK bars giving a wind-cheating forward lean, and found the bike 'rock-steady on long sweepers', with no over-the-ton weaving. Minus points included 'somewhat clashy' gears once the unit had warmed up, as well as noisy valve gear. The inaccessible light-switch, feeble horn (hardly surprising since it was mounted under the seat), and a lost silencer bolt were all mildly chided, but the vastly experienced Currie had become a confirmed fan of the model. Looking back a couple of decades later, he would write: 'If I had to pick out just one bike as *the* British bike of the 1960s, I would plump unhesitatingly for the Triumph Bonneville.'

The **1965** T120 addressed a number of the problems which had cropped up in the previous year. Within the engine, because of the occasional drive side main bearing failures, the crankshaft was now positively located on its drive rather than its timing side as previously. This was also aimed at reducing the rather rapid wear of the duplex primary chain. A new crankshaft timing pinion was fitted, butting up not to the inner spools of the main bearing, but to the outer face of the main bearing journal. The pinion also gave the clearance needed on the opposite side bearing. Also changed was the engine drive sprocket, which now butted up to the inner spool of the drive side bearing, not the end of the crankshaft's splines. In practice this drive side location would fail either entirely to cure the bearing failures, or to prolong primary chain life.

The electrical problems already mentioned had soon been joined by another, very serious one. The hard-to-adjust 4CA twin contact breakers caused a 'rogue spark' and pre-

A 1965 US T120R in classic Triumph colours.

ignition, which in turn meant piston skirt seizure and holed crowns. It became very important to employ a precise way of measuring TDC, and this was done by providing the means for stroboscopic timing. At the front of the '65 T120's right crankcase half, a plugged, threaded hole was provided, into which a small metal plunger could be screwed, which engaged with a slot on the flywheel when TDC was attained. Meanwhile, according to Dave Minton, 'those who knew' reground the contact-breaker cam to provide a 'slow' ramp behind the previously stepped cam; this eliminated contact breaker bounce and ensured reliability, even if timing accuracy was still impossible. Another factory dodge was to chamfer and radius the cylinder head gaskets at the cylinder bores, to help prevent pre-

ignition. Further electrical trouble-shooting included relocating the horn in a more audible position under the tank. For US machines, the tail-light became the pointed 'teat' type, or Lucas 679, but for that year only married to the previous number plate.

The engine finally lost the oil pressure indicator button with its two springs, which had been only marginally practical, as well as a prime source of leaks. It was replaced by a single spring-release valve behind a dome nut. In the gearbox, a felt washer was fitted behind the gearbox sprocket to keep out dirt. Mid-season, rear chain oiling was provided by a hole in the round cover plate behind the clutch, but being unmetered, the rear end and the rider's back got splattered, before the factory advised on how the hole should be sealed.

A '65 US Bonneville with shortie 'teardrop' mufflers.

Armstrong cork linings were fitted in the clutch.

From DU22682, the cylinder head's previously steel exhaust head adapter studs were replaced by alloy ones, but these were found to chatter and wear their threads away, causing weak running, so they would be changed back to steel the following year. Restyled, sweptback exhaust pipes were fitted for the T120R, and featured a bracing strap which connected the pipes directly, down by their bottom bend. UK models still fitted the long Resonator silencers, but for the US T120R, this was the first year of the short, pretty 'teardrop' silencers, which David Gaylin in his book correctly identifies as 'the classic sports muffler'.

For the cycle parts, the initially unsatisfactory

front forks were extensively revised to give more progressive damping, although they remained of similar appearance. An inch of extra travel was provided, by means of longer stanchions, sliders, internal damping sleeves and springs. The sliders no longer featured brazed-on fork ends, for the whole lower member was now machined from a solid billet of steel, with the front spindle revised to suit the new fork end's machined detachable caps. The headlight's supporting arms became longer, and rubber gaiters with closer pitches and a cleaner look were fitted. The optional qd rear wheel bearings changed from taper rollers to ball races. Both wheels were fitted with grease retainer rings and felt protective collars, but as Gaylin pointed out, in the US where bike use was more occasional, the felt trapped moisture during lay-ups and caused rust around axles and sealing rings. The swinging-arm spindle, which always need to be watched on Triumph twins, was now extracted from the more accessible right side.

Further detail changes included a redesigned, more upright prop stand, and a revised kick-start mechanism with a shorter kick-start ratchet pinion sleeve and thrust washer on the mainshaft, to help stop the pedal not returning fully. As mentioned, the previous year's unpopular kinked rear brake rod had been rerouted inboard of the left engine plate, with the rod now running behind the left shock absorber. The rev counter became a standard fitment for all T120 models, UK included.

The 1965 finish was one of the prettiest ever, with Pacific Blue tank upper and gold-striped Silver lower, and silver guards with a gold-lined blue stripe. This was the last year for the classic 'mouth organ' tank badges, and in the US, for the tank-top parcel grid. Seats on some US models became all black, and while T120R models sported mudguards of painted steel, almost all T120Cs had painted alloy front guards and painted steel rear ones. These 1965 twins were exceptionally good looking machines, and spearheaded a Sturgeon-led year which resulted in the company winning its first Queen's Award for Export.

The following year, **1966**, represented a major performance step-up for the Bonnie, and one that is remembered to this day – see the recollections of dealer and specials builder Bob Innes in Chapter 5. The T120R's claimed output was raised to 48bhp at 6,700rpm in the UK. As mentioned, the extra power came at the price of some peakiness and fragility. John Nelson would write that the '66 power characteristics were 'more brittle than before, and much more than many normal road-going riders came to care for', believing that what had been done

A '65 US T120 with 'slimline' tank, unreliable Smiths Magnetic instruments and (for the last year in America), a parcel rack.

A 1966 US T120R, 'disguised production racer', with famous 'white' handlebar grips.

Bonneville TT Specials

Another success story for 1965 was the Bonneville TT Special, which by the end of the year in the USA had won more events in its class than all other makes put together. TT aces Skip van Leeuwen and Eddie Mulder both won the first races they entered on the purpose-built Triumph, and they dominated the sport. Mulder won five AMA National TTs between 1965 and 1970, including all three in 1966, the TT's peak year, while 'van Looney' won four, and both were regular winners at the premier venue, clay-based Ascot Park.

As we have seen, since 1963 the TT Specials had been produced to JoMo's specifications, although they were supplied to both Coasts, and until mid-1966 they shared the T120C engine suffix with the other off-road sports Bonnies. However they were very different beasties, with 12:1 (said to be an actual 11.2:1) compression, 1⅜in carbs, batteryless ET (energy transfer) ignition, no lighting, a rev counter only, a 0–60 time of 5.5 seconds with top speeds of over 120mph (193kph), and an eventual claimed output of 54bhp. Triumph fitted the roadster's stands, dual seat and even the tank rack, although wise virgins removed the latter and blanked off its bolt holes. And in yet another example of Bonneville versatility, *Cycle World*

The flamboyantly gorgeous 1966 T120TT.

in 1963, observed that 'many people are buying this bike for ordinary street riding – and it is mild enough for that sort of running, too.' Even on the open downswept pipes it came with as standard, which as anyone will tell you who has ridden behind a T120TT when the taps are turned on and the dirty thunder of its exhausts explodes, blaring all over you – are LOUD.

Apart from the above, the specification remained remarkably close to the standard T120. Main change points specific to the TT were an 18-tooth gearbox sprocket for 1964, together with a huge Lucas S55 handlebar-mounted ignition cut-out switch practically large enough to operate with your forehead, and polished alloy guards. The following year saw the introduction of the classic 1¾in downswept twin short pipes tucked in under the crankcase, which meant the end of the centre stand. Compression dropped to a catalogued 11:1, and folding footrests were finally fitted. Some of the Eastern TT models contained an invisible but significant innovation, to counter a traditional Meriden problem. Their camshafts were 'tuftrided' to combat the rapid wear to which Triumph cams had always been prone, but John Nelson says that while this was all right for racing, there was a one-in-three failure rate under warranty when it was tried on roadster E3325 inlet cams. The ultimate

Eddie Mulder and a TT in action at Ascot Park.

factory answer would be Nitriding, but this effective treatment would only reach the Meriden production machines for 1969; although Doug Hele acknowledged benefiting from hardened cams on his 500 racers for 1966, after hearing about the process from TriCor men. Nitriding created some different problems. 'The process took 90 hours,' John Nelson recalled with amusement, 'so the boys on the camshaft line would hold the factory to ransom. And the Yanks didn't like it because you cannot weld extra lumps on to a Nitrided cam, so from then on, they had to make their own.'

For 1966, TT models entered the home straight with that year's slim tanks, hot engine and altered steering-head angle – although dirt racers preferred the previous year's 65° steering head. Both types however were well respected, despite many aftermarket frames like those from Trackmaster and Sonicweld being available. David Gaylin, in his book *Triumph Racing Motorcycles in America*, quotes Eddie Mulder: 'The TT Special was an excellent TT bike right out of the box … [with] one of the best chassis of any stock motorcycle. It was a rocket.' In mid-year the rocket adopted 'T120TT' engine prefixes. The last year of production for the TT was 1967, with stainless steel mudguards for both East and West versions. Around 3,500 TTs had been built in all, although the legend far exceeded mere numbers produced. Possible reasons for the model's demise ranged from the fact that most racers preferred to buy a used Bonneville and convert it themselves, to the company's wish to promote the far less suitable triples on the American tracks, to the disappearance by 1968 into the Vietnam maelstrom of many potential young TT riders. Whatever the reasons, the model may have been gone but it surely was not to be forgotten.

Downswept open exhausts were worth another 2bhp – but don't forget your earplugs! The fire-breathing T120TT, seen below in its final, 1967 form, was part of the Bonneville legend.

amounted to 'transforming a high-speed tourer into a disguised production racer.' This did not worry the many young Bonneville riders for whom speed was king; Gaylin comments on the improved throttle response, 'to the delight of wheelstand junkies everywhere.'

It was no coincidence that this was the year when sales-minded top executive Harry Sturgeon would really concentrate output on the US market. If a justification was needed, it would come in the sales figures for 1968–9, Meriden's peak year; when the Americans took 25,407 Triumphs, while the UK home market amounted to just 2,143. For 1966, Sturgeon's policy would win the group the Queen's Award for Export for the second time, but the man himself was to die tragically of a brain tumour early in 1967.

The 1966 hop-up started with compression raised to 9:1. The kick-start lever was even lengthened, to help cope with the extra bump. Internally, the crankshaft now reverted to timing side location, and on the drive side, the fitting of a heavy duty single lipped roller main bearing finally and effectively cured the problem of mains failure for several years. This crankshaft also featured a narrower flywheel, reduced in weight by a full 2½lb (1.134kg), with longer flywheel bolts, and with its periphery changed to a stepped section in order to maintain the previous 85 per cent balance factor. The lighter flywheel naturally made for an even more responsive engine, but at the cost of vibration 'peaks' from 5,000rpm increased in intensity. Vibration at speed became the tank-splitting variety. From DU29738, larger 1³⁄₁₆in Monobloc 389 carbs helped squeeze out the last ounce of power. Their float cover screws were set flush with the covers, so were no longer lock-wired, which had been a T120 visual signature from the start.

The engine also incorporated the race-developed camshaft and tappet changes as outlined in the 'Thruxton' section. Hele's development work had discovered that the 'Dowson' cams off the cooking 6T Thunderbird with their quietening ramps, if used in conjunction with high-performance 1⅛in radius R-type big foot exhaust cam followers, plus the Thunderbird's 'Red spot' inner and outer valve springs and bottom spring cup, to restrict valve bounce, gave longer valve openings and significantly better breathing. This was supplemented by positive pressure oil feed to the exhaust tappets and valve guides, by passages drilled in a hollowed dowel at the cylinder/crankcase joint and a revised timing cover. This helped, but did not eliminate, the Triumph's rapid camshaft wear.

In the head, steel exhaust adapter stubs were reintroduced, and those prime Triumph oil leak points, the pushrod tubes, became a type developed for the smaller twins, straight tubes with flared ends and new square-section silicone rubber sealing rings, top and bottom; a not wholly effective solution to the problem. Oil capacity was increased to six pints in a new tank with revised rubber mountings and a metered feed in its neck to the rear chain, with the previous over-enthusiastic feed from the primary chaincase being blanked off.

As well as the engine, the frame too, from early in the model year at DU25277, benefited from the race development. Hele's cure for continued high speed weave had been to steepen the steering head angle to 62° (the same as on Norton's Featherbed frame) by cutting and shutting the frame top tube and employing a new cast-iron head lug, thus achieving more trail while retaining the existing wheelbase. This also had the effect of putting the engine lower and more forward in the frame, giving a lower centre of gravity and reducing front end lightness. Later in the year, at DU27672, the steering lock was increased by modifying the lower fork yoke, to take advantage of the skinnier '66 petrol tanks and give an even tighter turning circle. The swinging-arm was also widened to allow the use of fatter tyres at the rear. Steering with the new frame could feel a little heavy, but in the opinion of *Cycle* magazine, the revised chassis 'set it head and shoulders above earlier models, especially in the area of handling and "roadability".'

Another aspect of a fundamental problem was tackled with a shift to 12-volt electrics, at first using two 6-volt batteries in series and then, from DU32994, a single battery, all of which meant revised battery platforms and fastenings.

The flamboyant 1966 US T120R Bonnie with Grenadier Red stripes, featured a steeper head angle.

The 12-volt system finally employed more satisfactory Zener diode voltage control, although initially there were teething troubles, as the diode was mounted on the inside of the left-side panel, out of the cooling wind. After failures due to the heat out West, from DU 32898 a new right-angled heat sink was employed. Other electrical improvements included a Yale-type ignition key, as the old pressed-steel spade keys meant the lock could be easily operated by a thief with a screwdriver. From DU31565, a Lucas 700 series headlamp shell fitted with ignition and main beam warning lights was adopted, although these early versions were completely obscured by the twinned instruments. On the right side of the handlebars came a huge kill switch with a chromed body, and for the T120R a brown button, although the TT models had a black one.

Another major trouble spot was addressed with a new front brake. This was still an 8in sls design, with a full-width hub, but with a new drum and shoes that gave a claimed 44 per cent increase in braking area. This had been achieved by mounting a vertical spoke flange on the right, which allowed the drum surface to be extended to the outside of the hub, at the same time as making it more rigid. This brake regularly stopped in less than the '30ft from 30mph' benchmark, although Hele with the racers was already working on something even better. At the rear, the brake on the standard, but not the qd wheel, whose sprocket had previously been integral, was again fitted with a bolt-on sprocket, a great aid to quick changes of ratio for sporting riders.

The rear wheels were also altered to accommodate a speedo gearbox drive, the change from the previous location on the engine's gearbox being an easier arrangement to replace. The rev counter drive also altered, still being taken from the exhaust camshaft but now on the drive side, via a right-angled drive exiting the left side crankcase, a less leak-prone arrangement than previously.

Without any obvious breaks with the past, the T120's appearance began to change subtly, starting with a Triumph signature, the tank badge. The good old 'mouth organ' had been very much a Fifties' fixture, while the new 'eyebrow' badges, so called because of the extended chrome furrows at their front end, while more modern looking, were also curiously effective jewellery. The Triumph logo was rendered in black surrounded by chrome and set on a white background. They were mounted on new slimmer petrol tanks, either 4 or 3 (Imp) gallons with glued-on knee grips for UK and general export models, but with a beautiful if impractical 2.5 (US) gallon teardrop tank, also with glued-on knee grips, for US T120R and TT Specials. These 'slimline' tanks, wasp-waisted at the rear, finally deleted the parcel rack, which like the tank badge represented one more link severed with the old Turner styling. But as Gaylin observed, the tiny tanks with little more than 100-mile range 'failed in every duty except one: no other single feature sold more Triumphs in the United States than that sensuous fuel tank.'

That year's colours were Grenadier Red and gold-lined Alaskan White, conventionally arranged with red uppermost on the UK models tanks. But on the tanks of US machines, white strikingly predominated, with just three-part red racing stripes along the centre and the top, as always divided by the chrome trim strip which concealed the tank's central weld. The '66 machines to start with also famously went out with 'white' (actually light grey) handlebar grips, but these were unpopular and were soon replaced during the model year with black ones.

With stainless steel mudguards front and rear, the US T120R, with a new polished cast aluminium tail-light housing for the L679 light, again for the US only, represented a significant step towards the final classical look of their best years. On all T120s the seat also changed its appearance, being the same basic hinged item, but with the rump kicked out by extra padding and a gold Triumph logo stencilled on the back panel.

The '66 Bonnies were enthusiastically received on both sides of the Atlantic. After lifting the front wheel in first and second, a *Motor Cycle Mechanics* test hit 94mph (151kph) in third and a top speed of 113mph (182kph). They found the bike could be laid over until the silencers grounded, and still stayed on line. Clutch, gearchange and the 'really powerful' 12-volt headlamp were also praised, as was the front brake. *Cycle World* judged that no other big sportster 'offers quite the same combined package of performance *and* reliability *and* handling'. As *Cycle* observed, 'because it can be brutally fast does not make it at all difficult to control.' Quite a trick to turn.

For **1967**, the T120's performance was tweaked again, together with some significant electrical improvements. With the death of Sturgeon, the all-out production and sales push continued under the new Group Chief Executive, Lionel Jofeh, who was to oversee the amalgamation of all US Triumph and BSA operations under one expensive umbrella during 1969. This not only turned away many key personnel with loyalty to one or other of the BSA or Triumph marques, but also undermined Meriden's profitability, by making the home operation liable for US warranty claims. This would happen at a time when the production mania meant that, even though the design of the Bonneville itself was nearing perfection, it was subject to, as Brooke and Gaylin put it, 'wild build quality variation'. Machines were

The Thruxton Bonneville

In the UK, Production racing, theoretically contested, on both short circuits and the Isle of Man TT course, by lightly modified versions of machines which the public could buy, was popular in Britain from the mid-1950s to the early '70s. Syd Lawton's Norton twins dominated the premier Thruxton 500 (mile) event until 1964, when with Doug Hele now at Triumph, Fred Swift and Percy Tait came second in the race, on a Lawton Bonnie. This was good news for Triumph riders, since as Syd Lawton said, Doug Hele regarded production racing as a means of improving the breed. The '64 success cued the name for the Thruxton Bonneville factory production racers, which were built in penny numbers during 1964 and 1965, theoretically for sale to the public.

In theory also, the special parts employed on them were to be available for sale too, but in practice, as John Nelson wrote, 'all the high performance parts being manufactured for distribution through the spares and service departments were instantly collared by Production and not replaced for nearly a season.' The Production races, 'a factory battleground' as Nelson called them, had become too important to the company for them to take their chances with genuine privateers; dealers were allocated the tweaked machines for favoured riders only. There was more; in many instances, even if you possessed the go-faster bits, unless they were assembled by Doug Hele's team with the know-how, they wouldn't go. The exhaust length, for instance, was crucial, and none of it had to protrude into the special silencer. The engines were also sensitive to the exact thickness of the carburettor induction rubbers, and so on.

Just eight Production race machines, with engine numbers running from DU10408 on, were prepared for dealers for 1964, in addition to the works bikes. Then, at the 1964 Show which was held in Blackpool, an Avonaire-faired machine was displayed bearing the Thruxton name, the forerunner of the limited number to be built for sale. The 'Big Build' of around 50 of these took place in May 1965, with just enough made to satisfy production race homologation requirements; their engine numbers running from DU23129 to DU23181.

The engines of these machines benefited from Doug Hele's race development programme, and beyond that from American know-how. The swept-back exhausts were linked by a cross-tube set as close as possible to the exhaust ports, which gave increased gas volume for each cylinder. This was in conjunction with the 1½in exhaust pipes being reduced to 1¼in, which significantly improved high speed gas-flow, as American tuners had long realised. The pipes had detachable mid-sections, as their tucked-in line blocked access to the primary

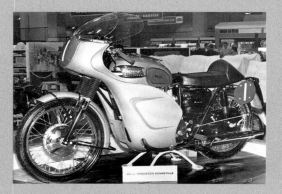

The T120 Thruxton, seen at the 1964 Earl's Court Show, was produced in very limited numbers for 1964–5.

drive and timing covers. The long silencers, with their distinctive rear hangers, contained a racing megaphone made for US dirt tracks and giving the best possible mid-range power.

Power was also boosted right through the range by the use, after much experimentation, of an existing touring-profile camshaft, E4220, from the Thunderbird 650, named 'the Dowson cam' after its designer. It was discovered that if used in conjunction with new valve springs and larger, 'big foot' 3in radius 'R'-type cam followers, the long opening and closing ramps, designed for quietness on the Dowson, provided longer valve-opening periods and greater lift. The exhaust cams featured positive oil feed. Most machines were supplied with close ratio gearbox internals, and geared quite tall. The carbs, as on early T120s, were chopped Monoblocs with a remotely mounted central float chamber hung between the instruments.

Hele steepened the frame's steering-head angle as

Much used and much modified, but rare, a genuine Thruxton Bonneville.

(Above) Malcolm Uphill on his way to win the 1969 Production Isle of Man TT race on a Bonneville racer, at an average speed of 99.99mph. (Right) Ray Pickrell laying a 650 over at Brands Hatch, 1970.

on '66 production T120s, and incorporated shuttle-valve damping in the front forks, of the kind that would appear on the standard bikes for 1968. The front brake was a ventilated version of the one on the 1966 production bikes. The machines were equipped with rear-set footrests and controls, a down-turned M-shaped handlebar, a humped racing seat, and 19in wheels front and rear for slightly better ground clearance. For weight saving, the badges were replaced by transfers. For the seven further machines built in 1966, alloy rims and a revised 'nosecone' Avon fairing were featured.

Not only did Triumph 650 Production racers continue to win at the 500 miler in 1965, '66 and in '69, but John Hartle took the big money Hutchinson 100 on one in 1967. Unlike Edward Turner, both the BSA/Triumph Group and Norton-Villiers, saw Production racing as part of their marketing policy, and partly as a result of this, a Production Isle of Man TT race was also inaugurated for 1967; John Hartle

won the top 750 class there for Triumph too, at an average speed of 97.10mph (156.23kph). But the peak came in 1969, with Malcolm Uphill's legendary Island victory at a 99.99mph (160.88kph) average which included a ton plus lap. That caused Dunlop to rechristen their K81 tyre the TT100. Triumph also won that year's FIM *Coupe d'Endurance*.

That was the Bonneville's racing peak, as for the factory, the triples then took over as the Group's flagship machines. But in the hands of privateers and dealer teams, the legend would continue on British tracks for many years to come.

Inside the '67 engine lay a redesigned oil pump and (eventually) strengthened Hepolite pistons.

A 1967 US Bonnie in psychedelic Aubergine Purple. This one is from early in the model year, and still equipped with Monobloc carbs, with that year's separate 'pancake' air filters.

being produced pell-mell in a factory increasingly subject to the demarcation dispute and wildcat strike excesses of strong, greedy, trade unions, and to dispiriting rumours about the BSA Group's intentions for Meriden. Yet from 1968 the bikes still became 'as good as they got'.

Another feature of these troubled years was the way in which, in the name of progressive engineering, changes and improvements were increasingly introduced in mid-year rather than at the start of the season. One prime example of this was the replacement of traditional British thread forms by the UNF system prevalent in America. This began during 1967 but would continue piecemeal for the next three years, and was never absolutely completed. The first candidates during the '67 model year were the gearbox, rear frame, and fuel tank mountings.

In the engine, the inlet camshaft became the same E3134 profile as the exhaust, but in this instance with the existing ¾in radius cam followers. As an interim measure, to counter the problem of wear, the camshafts were copper-plated, and there were two alterations to the cam followers' lubrication, first by a metered jet and then, from DU63043, by a timed system. The oil pump itself was redesigned to counter wet sumping, with an increase to the size of the scavenge plunger. Unfortunately, this led to a lowering of the oil level in the crankcase – which was not good for camshaft lubrication. Among other measures relating to oil-tightness, the pushrod cover seals were also modified yet again. From DU47006, the engine's con rods were increased in cross section. At DU44394, in a further move to streamline and rationalise production, Triumph had ceased to manufacture their own pistons, and Hepolite ones were fitted. There were initial problems with piston crown distortion, until the outside

specialist got the thickness right.

Another performance tweak involved the carburettors, first with the Monobloc 389s fitting larger (240) main jets, and then from DU59320, changing to 30mm versions of the new Amal Concentrics. In a first for the Bonneville, these instruments fitted choke slides, in conjunction with a conventional and convenient choke lever, handlebar-mounted on the right side. The US machines were now fitted with individual chromed circular 'pancake' air filters as standard, but UK ones still did not receive these.

Some significant electrical improvements were also seen in 1967. The 'rogue spark' had finally been run to earth (as it were) by increasingly desperate Meriden Service and Experimental personnel confronted with rough or non-running 650s. John Nelson has told me how Frank Baker had lain on his side on a rolling road to watch how a machine's contact breaker sparked as the points closed as well as when they opened. The trouble was traced to mismatched contact breaker cam profiles and spring tension, and although Lucas had been well aware of the problem, it was Meriden who pinpointed the cause. For '67, from DU51771, a new 160° dwell cam for the auto-advance unit was fitted.

This troubleshooting had previously been attributed by some, myself included, to Pete Colman of JoMo, but the major problem which Colman sorted out had involved closing the auto-advance range on the Energy Transfer ignition system fitted to some US competition variants. Colman also ensured that the pulse in their coils gave the optimum spark by effectively cutting a new keyway in the rotor. All of this represented an equally significant achievement to Meriden's, for the US market.

There was more. From DU49539, resin-encapsulated alternator stator windings were fitted, a major step in ensuring electrical reliability. From the rider's point of view, another bit of progress was the removal of the light switch from the left side panel to the headlamp shell, although this convenience was marred by the fact that it was the same circular switch, and very awkward to reach, being obscured by the twinned instruments, of which the speedometer had become the 150mph type. A slightly louder Lucas 6H horn was also fitted.

Among a host of other detailed changes, a new fork crown incorporating a steering head lock, and thick plastic handlebar grips are both worthy of mention, as was the move for UK machines to 3.00 x 19in front tyres to replace the previous 3.25 x 18in, and provide even sharper steering. Bracing for the exhaust pipes became two different strips attached to either side of the crankcase nose. A new dual seat was fitted, slimmer at the nose, with a horizontally cross-ribbed top surface and a slight hump separating the rider's portion from the passenger's. The top was still light-coloured, with white piping, and the grey bottom rim strip remained. In theory, the competition models' seats were all black, and by the end of the year this finish had displaced the grey on all US models. The new narrow-nose seat blended well with the wasp-waist rear of the 'slimline' tanks.

Overall colours for the year were a bit complicated. The UK models got a top tank section in Aubergine (deep purple, an appropriate shade for this most psychedelic of years), with gold-striped Alaskan White for the lower half and the mudguards with their gold-lined purple stripe. The US got a similar scheme but with the white-lined bright Gold as the second colour, and that year the mudguards on all US Bonnies were stainless steel. But the Californian sun was to turn the gold employed chalky within weeks, even in showrooms, so at DU48157, gold was replaced for them by Alaskan White. Fade-prone colours provided by Meriden were one of the American dealers' long-standing grudges, although a unit was actually set up on the factory roof to try to tackle the problem. According to Gaylin, because Meriden usually used the lower shade as a base colour, the Aubergine on these US machines became much lighter and lost its metallic shimmer when the gold was changed to white.

As well as the colours themselves, that year saw a change of the shapes in which they were applied. The upper colour was first based on the top of the 'eyebrow' tank badge. From the front of the badge it curved back on each side to meet on the top of the tank, forming a V just

The 1967 US T120R was another beautiful Bonnie.

beside the petrol cap. From the top rear corner of the badge the back edge of this coloured flash swept back and traced the shape of the knee pad, then curled under the pad's back corner and ended above the carburettors. But there was a different set-up on the TT's tank, with the lower colour coming down from the ends of the badges and its back edge curling under the knee grips. When the trouble was discovered with the gold finish, the US T120R also adopted this layout, as being less exposed for the lower colour.

Despite these shenanigans, the bike itself was a good one. A *Motor Cycle* test found the hot engine 'the smoothest yet', with a top speed of 110mph (177kph), but still tractable. The only qualification there concerned an irritating carburation flat spot just off the pilot jet, which resulted in some stalling at low speeds; it would be a year or two before the carburation would really be sorted. The brakes were judged excellent. Overall gearing, which UK and US T120R models shared, was found to be on the lowish side, so that the engine was really buzzing at high speeds. The combination of high footrests and a relatively low seat still gave a jockey-like riding position, but they got used to this quickly and found it to be comfortable. The steering still seemed light, with a suspicion of weave remaining above the ton. The feature they liked best was the acceleration – 'a solo which can out-rocket almost all other vehicles is not merely a useful bike but an exciting one'.

1968–70: the best years of their lives

A 1968 UK T120, with new forks. Note flashy brake drum cover and long Resonator silencers.

Triumph T120 Bonnevilles were clearly formidable motorcycles already, and now a series of thoughtful and timely developments lifted them to the very peak of their form. Most of the remaining problems – braking, electrics, camshaft wear and high speed handling – were significantly eroded by careful, often race-bred measures. Maybe it was because the Bonneville was replaced as Triumph's and the Group's nominal flagship during this period by the three-cylinder Tridents, or because from April 1968, it came up against an important evolutionary step in the story of parallel twins, the Norton Commando (with its anti-vibration rubber-mounted engine design permitting a 750 engine capacity to be employed practically), but in retrospect at least, there seems a poignant edge to these fine Bonnies. Their flames flared brightest just before near-extinction was heralded by Honda's CB750-4,

another 1968 *wunderkind* which would hit the UK the following year.

Although Meriden was producing bikes flat out, even then they were not meeting production targets, and selling everything they made. In the peak 1968–9 season, production rose to 37,059 with up to 900 machines a week being churned out, with engines and part-finished bikes accumulating in the aisles and yards of the factory, and sometimes machines were even shipped to the States with components missing. Meanwhile the misguided Group management, while attempting commonality of gearbox internals, forks etc with the BSA range, would also impose 'value engineering' ie no modifications if they would cost more than what they

The UK '68 T120 featured a 4-gallon tank with smaller knee grips but still with a parcel rack, and pullback handlebars.

replaced, while fragmenting the way forward with their notoriously mismanaged and expensive R&D centre at Umberslade Hall. Hele and Hopwood refused to participate, concentrating on the race programmes and on improving the product where possible.

It was from racing that the **1968** T120 displayed its most striking innovation, namely the 8in tls front brake and fully damped front fork, although the latter had a reassuringly similar appearance to its predecessor. The brake however stood out loud and proud, its size accentuated by a raised, polished rim strip around the brake plate, as well as an extended lip to the fluted, chromed brake drum cover on the other side. The latter was an unpopular feature which resembled a dustbin lid. The brake featured same-size shoes, and was well cooled via an air-scoop with a wire mesh at the front and an air vent at the back. The brake

cam levers were connected by an adjustable rod, with the cable swooping down from a clip on the right side of the front mudguard, down the guard itself, then looping in from the rear to an abutment cast in the brake backplate, through which it was threaded before continuing to the extended front cam lever. The first of three teething troubles associated with the brake was dealt with at DU70083 when the cable abutment was fitted with a split pin, to prevent a poorly adjusted cable jumping out of it. This was an extremely powerful stopper, probably the best production front drum brake the industry ever produced. A second, scary problem was the occasional instance, when the forks were fully compressed, the cable becoming trapped under the rear of the mudguard and jerking the brake on involuntarily. This was resolved mid-year at DU81709 with the fitting of a longer front mudguard, although this did not apply to the stainless steel guards on US models. For the brake, all that remained to be dealt with was a feeling of sponginess in its operation. The rear guard and lifting handles were also modified, with all guards now gaining a rolled edge at their ends. On UK models the painted stripe now stopped short of the end, with the pinstriping squaring it off.

The new forks featured Hele-designed floating shuttle-valves, giving true two-way damping. These shuttle-valves were attached to the lower end of the fork stanchions and were retained by a sleeve nut which also held the bottom bearing of the fork leg. One of the few external identifiers for the forks were the eight bleed holes above the bottom bearing location. T120R fork threads changed to UNF early on at DU68363, along with those on a new fork lower crown. These forks were a major improvement, their stiffened recoil damping meaning that Bonnies could now be laid over safely on the bumpiest of bends. Their increased travel was also a bonus on the dirt.

From DU68368, handling was also improved by a final Hele tweak at the other end of the machine, a new, longer swinging-arm (which meant a slightly longer rear chain), with heavier corner fillets for additional stiffness, and mounted on a new lug. Then at DU81196 the swinging-arm itself used a thicker tube section. Triumph swinging-arm lubrication had always been a problem, occasionally causing seized swinging-forks, which made their removal for renewal of bushes a difficult business, so the introduction of a breathing hole in the spindle to counter air locks while greasing, and a spindle sealing O-ring, were both welcome moves. The stiffened rear end, in combination with the new forks, made these the best-handling T120s yet.

In the engine, the inlet valve stems became Stellite-tipped, higher lift 'green spot' outer valve springs were used and Hepolite pistons with reinforced crowns were fitted. At the cylinder base, a long-standing maintenance problem was tackled with the introduction at DU75452 of 12-point bihexagonal base nuts, to provide better spanner clearance. Camshaft wear remained a problem, and from DU78400

The excellent new tls front brake, but with 1968's troublesome cable run and straight-pull action.

the oil feed to the rocker arm ball pins was cut off, to increase feed to the exhaust cam. There were detail changes in the gearbox to help oil-tightness, as well as gearbox selection modifications, with a new camplate plunger, spring and holder, although road tests would still mention low speed clonkiness. Externally the gearbox outer cover now came with a filler cap in its side, while the gear pedal rubbers lost their Triumph logo and became a plain rubber bulb, in common with those on BSAs.

In the electrical department, the big breakthrough was the change to Lucas 6CA contact breakers, on which the timing for each cylinder could now be set independently. Although there was more room on the points plate as the condensers had been moved to an independent mounting beneath the petrol tank, the new points still required a deeper chamber to house them, and thus a new timing cover. The points represented a major improvement, but the nylon contact-breaker cam could still wear rapidly, and the real, blessed solution would come in the 1970s with electronic ignition. Meanwhile, to facilitate the timing process, the T120's primary chaincase now featured a circular inspection plate fastened by

The great 'Mike the Bike' Hailwood receives his 1968
Bonnie from dealer Fred Green at a packed Thruxton circuit.

three screws and carrying an inlaid Triumph
logo painted in black. A timing plate could be
fitted in place of this inspection plate, and from
DU83021, a fixed pointer went on the
chaincase to align with a mark on the alternator
rotor while timing.

Further electrical improvements led off with a
new headlamp shell, within which the ammeter
was now silicone-mounted to help stop it going
open-circuit. The warning lights were
repositioned more visibly, and the headlamp
switch became a handy three-position toggle-
switch which the rider could flick on easily by
reaching forward. The Zener diode was finally
moved from within the left side panel to a
position out in the wind under the tank nose
where it sat is a finned heat-sink, all of which
effectively sorted voltage control. Another

practical touch came with the ignition switch
finally attaining an accessible position, near the
top of the left-hand fork cover.

With the diode and switch repositioned away
from it, a new left side panel was fitted, with a
tool compartment to replace the unpopular '66-
on underseat tray. The side panel was fitted
with new fastenings, although these proved
unreliable, and its single front screw fastener
was soon replaced by a threaded plastic knob
with a click-spring retainer. Unfortunately this
too was prone to letting go, and as Gaylin
observed, with the rather loud shortie US
mufflers, you couldn't even hear your toolkit
bouncing down the road! The US silencers,
incidentally, had their baffles redesigned to
combat loosening off. The steering head lock
was also revised, and the steering damper

eliminated for both the UK and US T120R, although a kit was available to fit one if desired. The US models' alloy tail-lamp housing acquired triangular red reflectors on its sides, with circular amber ones fitted under the front of the petrol tank, to comply with Federal regulations. The UK models kept the old tail-light, but their number plates changed to a rectangular shape. The prop stand was given a curved extension in place of its previous separate 'foot', and it now worked as well as the excellent centre stand. The UK petrol tank standardised on 4 gallons and fitted smaller, thicker knee grips as found on the smaller capacity twins. Air cleaners were still optional for UK models, but on the US machines, the circular air cleaners now came with threaded flanges to allow them to screw directly on to the mouth of the mixing chamber.

A new dual seat was fitted, with a chrome trim-band around its base. Still ribbed horizontally, which helped stop the rider sliding backwards under hard acceleration, it had thicker cushioning and revised hinges. On the US West Coast versions the mountings for the mandatory safety strap changed from curved rod to stepped strap hinges. Then late in the year the strap was replaced, at DU75452 for the West, 77018 for the East, with a short, chrome grab-rail, fastened directly to the rear of the seat. Colours for 1968 continued the previous year's psychedelic theme, with a metallic edge nodding at the burgeoning custom scene, being Hi Fi Scarlet and gold-lined Silver. UK tanks retained the '67 wings, but with their smaller knee grips now showing more of the silver, while US 'slimlines' were in solid scarlet, with a 2¼in wide gold-lined silver strip on top of the tank.

What was the profile of the US Bonnie man with his 100-mile gas tank? *Cycle World* the following year, testing the more practical TR6 Tiger single carb 650, acknowledged that both bikes had 'a pleasing tautness which separates them from other pushrod twins', but then compared the steadier Tiger to 'the cranky, fidgety-fast Bonneville. The stereotype Bonneville rider is a short-haul sort of guy who slicks his hair back and "gases it" incessantly.' Absolutely – that sounds like every rocker I ever knew. The magazine went on to acknowledge that 'the Bonnie is one of the few production machines capable of producing 100mph in the standing quarter, not to mention a 115mph plus top speed' and indeed, the UK's *Motor Cycle Mechanics* did hit 115mph (185kph) with their test '68 T120, as would the US *Cycle Guide* a couple of years later.

Cycle World would explore the Bonnie rider's identity a little more fully and precisely. 'The Bonnie has always been a status-cycle. The understated stud machine. Representative of Real Motorcycling … if you are a sporty rider and deem yourself a bit of a jockey … you know you are waiting for the day you can buy your Bonnie. Its image does not jibe with the purist. The Bonneville is more for the guy who would buy a Boss Mustang or a Z28. Performance-plus. Flashiness in a moderate way, and respectable handling. Like the

Meanwhile, you *could* put on your desert boots and safety helmet, and go touring, Bonneville style.

Sportster, the Bonneville is a stud bike, although the two images aren't quite the same.' This captures fairly perceptively the must-have quality of those fixated on Bonnies, and in these years it still applied to a lot of UK riders too. Commandos or CB750s notwithstanding, for them there would never be a roadburner like the T120.

For many, the Bonnie's finest hour was **1969**, both on the production race tracks, Isle of Man included, as well as in the quality of the bike itself. A 1969 *Motor Cycle Mechanics* test recognised that the changes to the model were progressive rather than dramatic, but observed that 'like a rare wine, you could say that the Bonnie improves with the years.' They also noted that 'somehow the characteristics of the motor have changed over the years and all the lumpiness which is associated with high performance machinery has been smoothed out to provide tractability at low speeds.' How this was done provides the key to the 1969–70 machines' top status, despite the arrival of the Trident as Triumph's nominal flagship.

The '69 model year severed yet another link with Triumph's past in adopting, in common with BSA, a new month-and-model-year engine number coding system (see Appendix for details). So it was at NC02256, or October 1968, that the major engine change took place: the fitting of a crankshaft with a heavier flywheel, although it retained the previous 85 per cent balance factor. At a stroke, the T120s 'fidgety-fast' feel was decisively modified, as John Nelson put it 'reducing the "peakiness" of the engine vibration', which, as he well knew had been bad enough to cause Meriden's Service Department on occasion to surreptitiously fit lower compression pistons and milder cams for worried UK customers, without their knowledge! The heavier flywheel evidently did not compromise the Bonnie's acceleration; the *Mechanics* test of a '69 T120 achieved a 6.4 second 0–60 figure, against a 6.8 second figure for the '68 test machine.

Meriden in conjunction with Amal also worked its magic on the twins' Concentrics. Several 1969 tests made specific mention of that year's clean carburration from tick-over on up, with the previous irritating flat spot, and

stalling, gone for good. Inside the carbs, the previously replaceable pilot jets were changed to fixed internal calibrated drillings. As for the stalling, an air bleed in the needle valve corrected the fuel mixture's inclination to go over-rich just before coming on to the main jet, while a flat spot just off the pilot jet was dealt with by tapering a previously parallel section of the needle. The dependable, non-stall carburation this produced was important at a time when Oriental machinery with push-button starting made sweating kick-starts while stalled at the lights the kind of embarrassment that could tilt a guy Eastwards. In addition, threaded carburettor inlet adapters were fitted in UNF sizes, as were the exhaust port adapters. The inlet adapter was tapered, from 1³⁄₁₆in to 1⅛in at the throat, a performance trick of which American tuners had long been aware. The carbs were now mounted on washers under the flange units featuring rubber O-rings. The Bonneville's main jets were reduced from 210 to 190, with the needle jets also reduced in size. The overall result was notably trouble-free carburation, although some would maintain that Concentrics reacted worse over time than the previous Monoblocs to a parallel twin engine's inherent vibration.

Another modification to the exhale side of the breathing, race-proved again, came with the fitting, close to the exhaust ports, of a link pipe between the two exhaust pipes. This brought benefits in two areas. Although less so than with race machinery on open megas, each exhaust benefited from the extractor action in the other pipe, and this gave better low and mid-range running. More significantly for the road rider, because parallel twin cylinders fired alternately, the link pipe meant each exhaust phase was absorbed by both silencers rather than just one. The result was described as 'phenomenally quiet' in a test on a '69 Tiger, and thanks to this, UK models that year could adopt as standard the sexier short US mufflers in place of the previous long Resonator silencers.

The UNF changeover continued, resulting in new timing and primary covers, and these also had wider joint faces. The incontinence of Triumphs and BSAs was still a standing joke Stateside, where in addition to drip trays,

Pretty near as good as they got – the '68 US T120R.

Triumph stockists were reported to market 'a device to be clamped onto the bottom of the frame that has some absorbent material to collect [the] oil'! Meriden also tackled oil-tightness for '69 with still another change of pushrod tubes, the new ones featuring serrated castellated top ends and Viton O-rings top and bottom; these were then modified mid-season with a further rubber washer at the bottom.

The majority of nuts, bolts etc, although not all, changed to UNF for this year, making this period a bit of a minefield for restorers. One example was the rev counter drive from the crankcase, which not only went UNF but also changed to a left-hand thread, so that road shocks tightened rather than loosened it off – but as Gaylin pointed out, 'many crankcases were ruined by Saturday afternoon mechanics attempting to fit early tach drive units or plugs

with previous threads!' On the left-side crankcase, just below the cylinders where the engine number was stamped, there was now a raised pad stamped with tiny Triumph logos, to discourage number-fixing.

On the lubrication front, the oil pump received a larger diameter feed plunger in a new pump body. The redesigned oil pressure release valve with UNF threads was also necessary since 1969 brought an electrically operated oil pressure warning light in place of the old tell-tale button, although this proved temperamental in the heat, and caused far more rider anxiety than it was worth. A more useful tweak came at DU44394 when the oil level in the crankcase was raised by making the scavenge pipe slightly shorter. A useful rider touch was the fitting of a dipstick to the oil tank's cap. Another real milestone came from

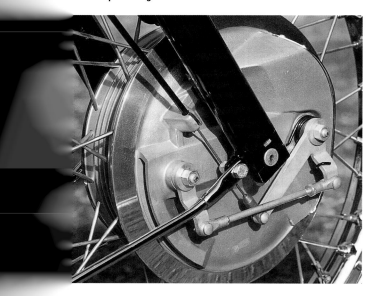

DU87105 when the object of many previous
lubrication mods, Triumph's wear-prone
camshafts, were finally sorted by their being
surface hardened by the Nitriding process. This
was also applied to Service replacement cams
for earlier model years, the clue in all cases
being a stamped 'N'.

The gearbox benefited from wider
transmission gears, now also subjected to a
hardening process. Third gear was lowered
slightly. During the year there were several
further changes to the selection process, as
well as gearbox shafts with different diameters,
but none of the new components was
interchangeable with the previous ones. From
DU88333 the clutch was given a statically
balanced housing, to combat transmission
vibration. A *Cycle* test that year found a 'satin
feel' to the clutch operation, but other tests
noted that 'the gearbox still grinds' when going
into first from neutral. As we shall see, this
would lead to a further ill-conceived attempt to
improve selection.

On the electrical side, a higher output RM21
alternator was fitted, and the 6CA points

modified with a second oil-seal as well as a
pre-lubricated spindle. The wiring harness had
provision for direction indicators now, and to
comply with US legislation, the front brake
cable incorporated a brake-light switch. The
only retrograde step around this time was the
use of German-made Siba coils on some
T120s, which reacted badly to West Coast
heat; in fact they melted! But for the rider, the
big innovation was the fitting, on the front
downtube, of a pair of horns which could finally
get a car driver's attention, the excellently loud
twin Windtones. These were heavy enough to
stress their mountings, which had to be
reinforced in mid-season.

On the cycle side, the front fork gaiters were
now the clipless variety, while the forks
themselves were widened a little to allow fatter
tyres to be fitted, and had a longer spindle. A
new front mudguard was fitted, with its rear
stay reverting to a single-bolt fixing. More
significantly, the spongy feel of the TLS front
brake was tackled by a final major modification.
The cable, after routing through a grommet in
the right headlamp bracket, was now run
vertically down the fork leg to a new operating
mechanism, with a redesigned abutment for
the end of the cable, which then led to an
altered front cam lever. The lever was bell-
cranked, instead of being straight, so that it
could be worked by an upward pull from the
rerouted cable, rather than a rearward one as
previously. On the other side of the wheel, the
'dustbin lid' cover plate was changed to a
cleaned up design with a pattern of concentric
rings. *Cycle Guide* called the results 'a front
binder that is really superb'.

Overall the T120's appearance was cleaned
up a little in unobtrusive ways. The 'eyebrow'
tank badge gave way to a simpler 'picture-
frame' design, and for UK models, the tank-top
grille was finally deleted. The dual seats were
now fitted with aerated tops, and those for the

UK became all-black like those in the USA. The rear units lost their shrouds and came with the exposed springs which all young riders wanted, impractical or not. The '69 colour scheme was trendy Olympic Flame (a more orange shade than the previous scarlet) and white-lined Silver, with the colours arranged as for 1967–8 on UK machines, but the US again undergoing three variations before settling on a classic configuration.

For 1969, US mudguards ceased to be stainless steel and became painted again, and when this was so the mudguard stays, previously black, usually became chromed, although the UK models stuck with black stays. The guards for both were silver, with a white-lined Flame centre strip. The first US colour scheme was arranged in the same way as the previous year, but soon after, for the tank this was changed to the first true 'scalloped' design – shapes which had originated with Gurley, a US custom painter, in the mid-1950s. On the top a thin flash of white-lined silver started from the top corners of the tank badges and curved backwards, tapering to a point on either side of the top seam. In the third, and most common version, this was joined by a lower flash starting from below the badge's bottom corners, and tapering to a point under the front of the knee grip.

Magazine testers on both sides of the pond appreciated the improved '69 machines, although with a young Sixties' readership they had to be more realistic than their predecessors. *Motor Cycle Mechanic*'s bike suffered from a dragging clutch and all they could say about the 12-volt headlight was that it was better than a 6-volt one. The horn/dipswitch on their T120 also let in water and one night shorted out, setting off the Windtone horns! *Cycle Guide* the following year mentioned that 'grinding' gearbox, a couple of spots of oil on the floor when their T120 was left overnight, and mechanical noise,

The veritable Gurley-derived 'scallops', seen here on a 1970 US T120R.

although they judged that to be 'merely a sound of machinery doing its job'. But a feeling of fondness for the Bonnie, as the Trident and Honda crowded in on the wings, pervaded these reports. The traditional easy starting, good traffic manners, excellent brakes and handling, piled up points for the T120, but the heart of the matter was elsewhere, summed up with an affecting simplicity by *Cycle Guide*'s man: 'The Bonneville has a great deal of personality … This is one of those things that kind of grows on you. The more you ride it, the more you like it … For sheer feel it's very difficult to find anything better than the Bonnie. This feel is what endears itself to the owner …'

Comparatively few changes were introduced for 1970, as the new wholly Group-owned US subsidiary sent itself into hock with the triple-led race effort, as well as leaching profitability with warranty claims which now had to be met by the factory direct. The Group got deeper into debt with the banks, and relied more and more on its motorcycle side, at the same time as missing substantial parts of the vital US selling season. This was due to disruption from

As beautiful and purposeful-looking as ever, but in 1970 the Bonnie was coming to the end of its good days.

Revised engine breathing, with a thick tube exiting to the rear of the primary chaincase. Note also the large Windtone horns!

poorly executed attempts to modernise production, and from industrial action by the Meriden workforce who both knew their own bargaining strength and were increasingly discontented and fearful about BSA Group management. Group boss Lionel Jofeh fuelled these fires by telling a mass meeting that he would close the factory if productivity, already stretched to the limit, was not increased, and by authorising the rough Umberslade-designed beast that was the coming Bonneville, to slouch towards Meriden.

So **1970**, a peak sales year in the USA, was for many to be the last year of the 'real' T120s, and it was mostly a good one. One major innovation improved the engine breathing, which in turn meant significantly better crankcase oil-tightness. The crankcase now breathed directly into the primary chain case via three holes drilled in the crankcase wall below the drive side main bearing housing, with the bearing no longer fitting an oil seal either. The previous timed breather was deleted. At the rear of the primary case, a new breather elbow, bolted on externally, took a large bore pipe which ran back to the top left of the rear mudguard, with the rise in the pipe stopping excess oil venting to atmosphere. The system was simple, and it also maintained a constant level of oil within the primary chaincase. It did mean new (UNF) camshafts, lacking the previous breathing set-up, were required, which in turn meant new crankcase halves. The latter proved substantially oil tight.

Oil tightness was also pursued in the gearbox, with the inner cover modified so that a shorter selector rod, less likely to provide a leak-point, could be fitted. The selector forks became aluminium-bronze with integral rollers at ED51080. But then disaster struck with a replacement for the previous camplate, plunger and indexing spring. The story merits a little detail, as it provides a concrete illustration of

This shining 1970 US Bonneville is actually one of the rare T120RT 750s produced in America for homologation purposes.

the basis for Meriden's fears that incompetent Group interference could directly affect Triumph's product, good name and profitability.

Alan Sargent was working at that time as Engineering Manager at Umberslade Hall ('the only good thing' he said, 'about setting up Umberslade/Slumberglades/Disneyland was that it finally gave the three Group factories, Small Heath, Meriden and Redditch, one thing they could all agree to despise!'). The place's lack of definition, according to Alan, deepened most disastrously with the appointment of a Divisional Quality Manager, 'who was no more a quality manager than an eggshell. It's a good idea to try to make quality part of the engineering process; it's a bad idea to appoint a disaffected factory superintendent from a nearby industrial town, deeply resentful that he wasn't a superintendent any more.'
Umberslade's boss, Mike Nedham, 'was a nice guy, but coming from the aircraft industry, he'd had no experience of Midlands-type industrial

people, who could be pretty tough hombres. He lacked the will to enforce his directives with this uncouth bugger, who dominated everybody and did awful things.'

And one of these concerned the Triumph gearbox. The Quality Manager's efforts in pursuit of neat production engineering caught up with the unit gearbox camplate, when he heard about a Hoffman fine blanking precision tool, which in theory was sharp enough to stamp the gearbox camplate all in one go; this camplate would then be operated by a leaf spring. But Hoffman, when approached, said the amount of metal between the external profile of the cam and the internal profile of the détente was too thin, so that it would twist. 'So the Quality Manager,' Alan told me, 'decided to put more metal in; he changed the profile, and conned Brian Jones into changing the drawings – he was really very uncouth, presumably he frightened Brian into doing it.'

The new camplate with leaf spring got into

production in mid-1970 at ED52044, 'before anybody in the system knew about it – and initially it often changed 1½ gears at a time. We had to spend an awful lot of time, which we couldn't spare, to stop it doing this, by juggling spring rates etc.' In addition the mechanism proved very difficult to refit during a rebuild, and swelled warranty claims from then until mid-1973, when it was finally replaced.

Otherwise it was detail changes only. The front engine mountings changed to bolted-on plates rather than welded-on, mainly to speed assembly. The front mudguard mounting lugs were altered, and the lower stay attached by two bolts, not one, since both front and rear guards were now common to all the twins, and this involved another revised rear number plate. The lengths of the front fork stanchions on which the sliders bore were now hard-chrome plated and ground to a micro-finish to prolong seal life (and to provide a sick comparison with the following year's offering). New Girling rear units were fitted, with a castellated protective collar for their three-position adjusters.

The Concentric carburettors were improved again by the fitting of a handy drain plug for their bowls. Larger, dome-shaped Windtone horns were used, and at ED44339 restriction plates were added to their slotted mountings to stop them slipping and hitting the front mudguard. The width of the UK model's ribbed

front tyre went from 3.00 to 3.25 inches. The base of the handlebar control lever was altered to allow mirrors to be fitted. For both UK and US models, a new combined grab-rail/lifting handle was introduced, joining to the rear mudguard mounting loop. This portion was black on early 1970 machines, with the grab-hoop chrome, but later in the year it changed to all chrome. The rev counter drive changed from a push-fit to a solid screwed-in plug in the exhaust camshaft. In mid-season, the Smiths magnetic instruments with grey centre circles changed to black-faced ones. Smaller, lighter Lucas ignition coils were fitted. A new dual seat pan lowered its height a little. The centre stand was modified and so was the prop stand, which now included a welded-on threaded boss for an adjustable stop-screw to help stop the stand clanging on the silencers.

Colours were still red and gold-lined silver, but this year's red was a beautiful metallic maroon dubbed Astral Red. Mudguards were red with a gold-lined silver stripe, and while the tanks of the US machines stayed with those sensual scallops, the big UK tank featured a less imaginative silver oval side-panel encircling, rather than using, the shape of the knee grip.

But as I found in Chapter 1, it still looked pretty good. In fact it was hard to fault a 1970 Bonnie. *Cycle Guide* that year may have called the styling 'a bit on the garish side, but in a pleasant way'; however they confirmed that '. . . even with the introduction of … more exotic and stronger running machinery, the Triumph Bonneville is still the 'in' bike with the local drive-in crowd. They are the most commonly seen and most-sought after piece of merchandise by teenagers …' The Bonnie's natural rival on the street had always been Harley-Davidson's Sportster, particularly in XLCH form. The 883cc Harleys were more expensive, some 100lb (45kg) heavier, didn't

'Do not go gently . . .' The US T120RT stood proud.

handle as well and could be harder to start, but for some there was no substitute for the rolling thunder of their vee-twin motors, which if not totally reliable at least had a certain agricultural ruggedness (and a magneto). Real outlaw riders, the 1 per cent patch clubs, favoured stripped and chopped versions of the bigger Harley 74s, but as Hunter S. Thompson in 1966 pointed out in his definitive book *Hell's Angels*, 'the Sportster, the Bonneville and the BSA Lightning Rocket … will run circles around a stock Harley 74, and even the Angel version of the hog – which is anything but stock – can't run with the newest and best production models without extensive alterations and a very savvy rider.'

The Sportster however was something else, appealing to somewhere between a Triumph rebel and a full-on outlaw, and presenting the Bonnie with a good match. As *Cycle* put it in 1969, the T120 was 'very much like the Sportster in lots of ways … both machines somehow add up to more than the sum of their parts, both are sexy and fast with big reputations to defend, and both are highly visible.' *Cycle* reckoned the two camps respected each other, 'for probably no reason save that of knowing that the other guy could blow him off if his bike was sharp. Sportster guys don't intentionally mess around with Bonneville guys at stop lights; Bonneville guys don't often ask Sportster people if they want to

go a couple of blocks for pink slips either. Mutual respect from mutual fear.' They noted that despite the 200-odd cc capacity difference, examples of the machines they had had on test had been pretty evenly matched over the standing quarter; 13.65 seconds and a terminal speed of 97.29mph (156.54kph) for a recent Shovelhead Sportster, and 13.88/96.90 (155.91) for a '69 Bonnie with just 100 miles on the clock. If a Triumph did blow a Harley hog away, this was known as 'smoked ham'.

Great days in a great, youthful decade. With new AMF management, the Milwaukee Marvel was about to go through some turns, but it was nothing to what the imminent future held for Triumph. Meanwhile in the near-perfected T120, Meriden had something of which to be justly proud. Both British and US fans could identify with regular track victories like Malcolm Uphill's '69 win on the Island and Triumph dirt dominance on Ascot's half-mile, against real opposition from 750 Nortons and XR-750 Harleys respectively. Their machines could benefit from tuning lore built up from these endeavours and from dedicated dealers who really knew the strengths and weaknesses of Meriden's ever-evolving product. For, as *Cycle Guide* concluded in 1970, 'there is a lot to be said for improving the breed and the Triumph Bonneville is an excellent example of just what this term means.'

As *Cycle World*'s Peter Egan would write in a retrospective piece, by 1970 Triumphs were 'a cultural icon … as much a part of the American scene as James Dean, '51 Mercs and Lucky Strikes.' The '67–'70 Bonnies, he concluded eloquently, 'seemed, like the DC-3 aircraft or the Winchester saddle gun, to be the final product and distillation of everything learned about balance and proportion in the era that preceded it.'

And then, alas, it was time for a big change again.

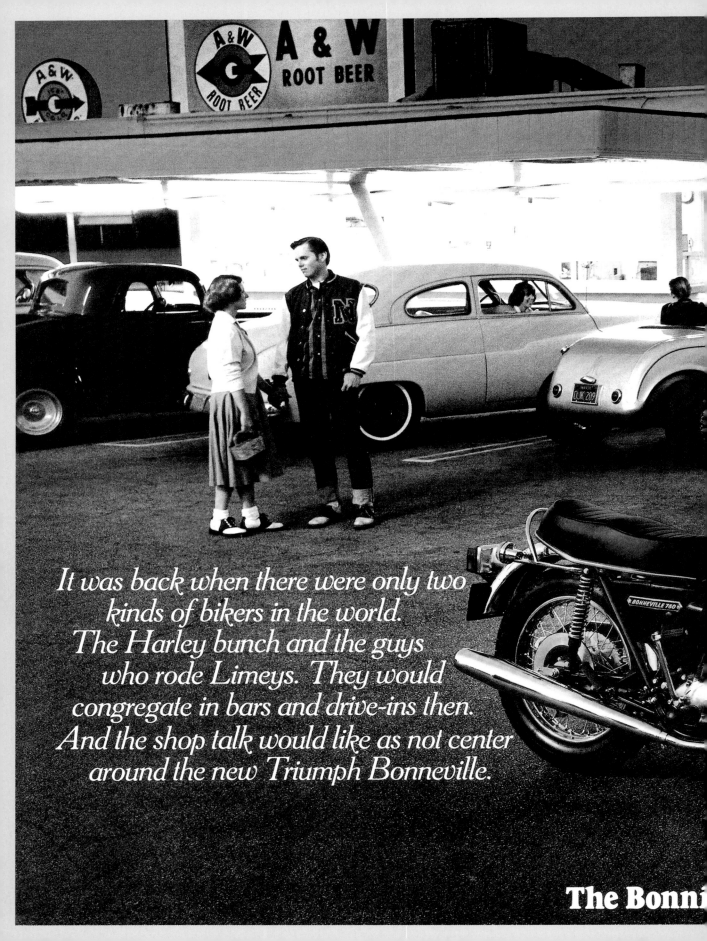

*It was back when there were only two
kinds of bikers in the world.
The Harley bunch and the guys
who rode Limeys. They would
congregate in bars and drive-ins then.
And the shop talk would like as not center
around the new Triumph Bonneville.*

The Bonni

It was known as the Bonnie. The production hot rod of the motorcycle industry. You couldn't mistake that unique profile—the streamlined look of its lean frame, its powerful vertical twin engine and its distinctive tank.

The Bonneville had class.

It was light, stable, with incredible acceleration. And the guy who rode one had an understandable attitude of superiority. He knew that he had the most responsive, best handling motorcycle ever built.

The Bonneville has proven to be a legend in its own time. And the legend continues. Others have tried to copy it for 20 years, but haven't come close.

Today, you can still enjoy the classic styling, the raw power and the unmatched handling that sets the Bonnie apart.

Why wait? Make your own legends, now.

hey never forgot it.

The handsome 1970 T120RT lump looks like a 650 but conceals high bump pistons and 750 hop-up.

1971–88: The long goodbye

In 1966, Edward Turner had confided in TriCor's Don Brown that in his view, the design of his ground-breaking parallel twins had been obsolescent for at least 12 years.

He was not alone in thinking this, as many at Meriden were well aware that with the immensely popular 48bhp Bonnevillle, they were flying high on shaky wings which had just about reached their performance ceiling. Malcolm Uphill's team-mate for the famous 1969 Production TT victory, Rob Gould, had retired with a broken crankshaft in his Bonnie, and on the American dirt tracks, top tuner Danny Macias recalled how he would carry out a full internal inspection of the T120TTs in his charge every two races, because 'we broke a lot of crankshafts, until I started Magnafluxing them between races.'

This is not to say that the '68-on Bonnies were not fast enough for most road riders, and their reassuring continuity and rider friendliness would have assured a long and happy future in their current form. But something, clearly, would also have to be produced to take on the new generation of Japanese superbikes, and despite its racing successes, the Trident, heavy,

thirsty, expensive, and not too reliable, did not seem to be it. Leaving aside the fact that, due to a complicated engine production process, it could never be built in sufficient numbers to be profitable. But with talent like Hele and Hopwood at Meriden, alternative designs would be laid out, including a new short-stroke parallel twin in the currently hot 750 capacity and complete with a balancer linkage.

That, however, was not the route which the BSA Group chose to take. As far back as 1969 it had been announced at Small Heath that the way forward would involve completely revised running gear for the existing engines. Since the new chassis were to emanate from the uncoordinated R&D centre at Umberslade Hall, it was no surprise that the launch of the 1971 BSA/Triumph range, including the new T120R, would prove anything but a smooth process.

When the drawings for the new P39 oil-bearing frame arrived at the production stage, it was still not right. As Alan Sargent recalled, 'when the jigs for the oil-bearing frames arrived at the two factories, they weren't to the drawings. The Small Heath (BSA) Works Manager talked about altering the drawings. But

When a Bonneville m the world moves too.

1971 is a good year for Triumph followers!
Triumph Power Plan 1971 means new
machines with a host of new features
including competition-type brakes, a lighter
yet more rigid frame, new competition-type
forks for improved control, new flashing
indicators and switch consoles. These

improved specifications mean better
handling and performance. Styling changes
mean striking good looks!

650 cm³ Bonneville. The most famous
Triumph of them all. Programmed development has made this machine the world's mos
consistent production race victor for its class
Now the new Bonnie comes with new brakes,
new frame combining strength with lightness
new forks and other exciting new features.

oves,

Did someone have a sense of humour about 1971 oil-in-frame vibration?

750 cm³ Trident. This machine took 15 records at the 1970 Bonneville Speed Week, won the Bol d'Or at a new average speed, won the Isle of Man Production TT and claimed a hatful of North American victories! Now restyled for exciting appearance, the new Trident comes with fade-free brakes, new forks and many other features.

650 cm³ Trophy. The new Trophy offers the mechanical simplicity of the single carburettor unit with twin cylinder power. The competition-type forks give more positive handling. The new frame is immensely strong and carries the engine oil. The new design incorporates a twin upswept exhaust system with a chromium-plated heat shield, together with a crankcase shield. Trophy 650 . . . Triumph know-how at its best.

500 cm³ Daytona. Remember the 500's that beat all-comers for two years running in America a few years ago? Remember the name of the race? Daytona! The new machine has the same basic power unit (twin cylinders, twin carburettors), giving the sort of performance which brought success in that classic race. Only now it's even better!

250 cm³ Trail Blazer. When the going gets tough – that's when the Trail Blazer is really at home. From the rugged proving ground of competition successes, Triumph have produced new forks and a power unit in a new lighter but stronger frame. New features such as the quickly detachable lights for competition use show that the Trail Blazer is ready for work any time, any place.

TRIUMPH

THE QUEENS AWARD TO INDUSTRY 1967 1968

Triumph Engineering Co. Ltd.,
Meriden Works, Allesley, Coventry CV5 9AU.
Telephone : Coventry 20221 – Meriden 331

at Meriden they took a jig and cut and welded it until the frame it would produce was correct'.

The problem was quite fundamental. While the short-stroke BSA 650 engines would fit in the frame, the taller T120 motors would not. The result was that, after the much smaller numbers of still conventionally framed 500 Triumphs for 1971 had been built, production at Meriden, which was all twins and triple assembly, ground to a halt for three long months, from October 1970 on. To fit the 650 motor into the P39 chassis, the cylinder head had to be redesigned by Meriden, as although the engine could just be fitted into the frame if the rocker boxes were removed, once it was in, the boxes could then not be secured again! All this meant that with production only beginning in January 1971, the new models missed a large part of the US selling season.

The redesigned T120 cylinder head to fit the P39 frame. The additional side holes helped tappet adjustment.

The oil-in-frame

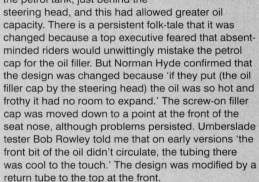

The all-welded P39 frame had been designed by Dr Stefan Bauer, who had also laid out the initial Norton Commando chassis. It consisted of a large 3in x 16 gauge central spine tube running back from the steering head and bending downwards to form the seat tube. Like the sports frames produced by the Rickman brothers in the UK and by Trackmaster in the US, and both frequently fitted with Triumph motors, this frame, in that thin-walled central section, carried the engine oil. While justifiable on weight-saving grounds in short-haul competition machinery (the Trackmaster saved 15lb/6.8kg on the standard pre-o-i-f Triumph chassis), it was a dubious move for potentially long distance road-going machinery.

Umberslade's Chief Stylist, Steve Metham, wrote recently that he had suggested the arrangement because 'you now have "for free" all the space once occupied by an oil tank,' and that this was of particular benefit for a project to reduce induction noise for the new range of machines, with pipes, filters and plenum chambers to be accommodated. The new design certainly did not free up any useful space for the rider; its side panels with their dummy louvres did not open, and this meant that the toolkit was squeezed back in under the seat, and that access to the battery was no longer available from the side.

More significantly, oil capacity dropped from 6 to 4 pints, and from then on Bonnevilles ran hot. Experimental Department man and Triumph specialist, Norman Hyde, has written that although Hele's men had a thermometer which they had used to do the Trident oil cooler tests, 'when it came to the

Bonneville we had to buy a new thermometer because the factory one didn't go up high enough! When we did our first test with a hot engine it was like something out of Tom and Jerry – the mercury shot straight off the end of the scale.' Oil coolers have been an advisable fitting of o-i-f Bonnies ever since.

The original frame design had the oil filler cap in front of the petrol tank, just behind the steering head, and this had allowed greater oil capacity. There is a persistent folk-tale that it was changed because a top executive feared that absent-minded riders would unwittingly mistake the petrol cap for the oil filler. But Norman Hyde confirmed that the design was changed because 'if they put (the oil filler cap by the steering head) the oil was so hot and frothy it had no room to expand.' The screw-on filler cap was moved down to a point at the front of the seat nose, although problems persisted. Umberslade tester Bob Rowley told me that on early versions 'the front bit of the oil didn't circulate, the tubing there was cool to the touch.' The design was modified by a return tube to the top at the front.

This was not the end of the P39's problems, however. The manufacturing process was new to Meriden and Small Heath welders, and early examples were dispatched with split, leaking seams or more frequently, welding cack within them, ready to circulate with the oil and wreck the engine. US Group Service men devised a pressurised flushing pump, and before long Meriden adopted something similar. There was more; the poorly designed over-long centre stand was not only extremely awkward to operate, but its pivot cross-tube was attached directly to the bottom of the frame's main oil-bearing spine, and when it twisted in use could crack and fracture the frame, causing oil leaks around the sump filter. The prop-stand lugs were also known to rip out of the frame. For this same reason, fitting crash bars or a sidecar to the o-i-fs was deemed inadvisable.

Finally, one main rationale for adopting the chassis, namely weight-saving, seemed to have misfired, as in contrast to the pre-o-i-f T120's claimed 363lb (164.6kg) dry weight, the new 1971 machine was catalogued at 387lb (174.2kg) dry. However, since one was weighed in for a *Cycle World* road test in May 1971 at 399lb (181kg) *kerbweight*, which is normally over 20lb (9kg) heavier than dry weight, the catalogue for once seemed to be selling the new bike short. It certainly felt light for a 650.

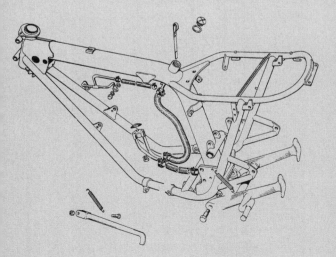

The oil-in-frame layout.

1971 to 1973: Disaster and recovery

The most universally striking motorcycle event of 1969 had arguably not been Malcolm Uphill's Island victory or even the arrival of Honda's CB750, but a movie – *Easy Rider*. Its popularity meant that the chopper cult which had been simmering healthily in the States now became a mainstream phenomenon. This explains a lot about the style of the **1971** Bonnies, which initially all went out as US spec models. They retained much of the classic Triumph look, with black frames and side panels, white-lined black scallops on their metallic mustard Tiger Gold petrol tanks, which continued to sport the 'picture-frame' tank badges, and short painted Tiger Gold mudguards with a white-lined black centre stripe. But the quite high, very wide bars, skimpy mudguards, the naked fork stanchions' kicked-out look at the front (although the actual steering head angle remained at 62°), the new short megaphone-style silencers, the flat high-mounted headlamp's small profile and a certain spindliness to the twin downtube frame, all nodded to the fashionable chopper scene.

Unfortunately, however, the low-rider element was not possible with the P39, which in the Triumph version featured a whopping 34½in (876mm) seat height (although this was catalogued at 3in less). The tall riding position was aggravated for shorties by the redesigned dual seat with its broad, squared-off nose; visually this also married awkwardly with the narrow rear of the new, fatter-at-the-front 3.5 (US)/2.75 (UK) gallon tank, which featured a simplified BSA-type single-bolt centre fixing. Talking to a Meriden tester, Colin Smith, he confirmed that 'I'm medium height at 5ft 8in and I couldn't touch the floor on the '71 oil-in-frames'. Many shorter riders on both sides of the Atlantic found the same.

The duplex downtube frame with its immensely stiff spine otherwise performed well in conjunction with the new Ceriani-like front forks pivoting on top-notch Timken needle roller bearings. These all-alloy forks featured internal damping by clack-valve, and provided 6in (152mm) of movement, which in conjunction with softer 110lb (49.9kg) rate Girling units at the rear, gave a markedly more comfortable ride at the cost only of fractionally less precise steering than previously. At the outside of the performance envelope, the notably long, thinner swinging-arm was prone to some flexing, but overall handling and roadholding with the new set-up were more than acceptable.

Given the fact that the engine and electrics were still the relatively well-sorted ones as before, is it fair that the 1971 650s continue to be so universally disdained, as reflected in their low price today compared with T120s from the Sixties? A detailed comparison with what had just passed may help explain why. The front forks looked sexy and worked well, but their exposed gaiterless stanchions rapidly let dirt burst their oil seals and they gushed liberally after that, despite changes to the seals, so the previous items were much more functional.

Between the forks sat not the disc brake

The 'comical' hub brake – but it was not funny when it went out of tune.

needed to keep up with the Japanese Joneses, but a new, 8in alloy conical hub tls front brake, with a massive air scoop mostly only good for letting in rain water. Both the brake's short cam levers were operated by the cable, the front lever being pulled on by the cable end, and the rear one squeezed on by the cable's casing; but with time, despite original cables being as thick as a speedometer's, the casing inevitably compressed. Initially the portion of bare cable between the arms had a black plastic sleeve, but this was replaced by a spring. As a result of the design, Meriden's Colin Smith commented 'Service got endless complaints about its sponginess, which we testers had pointed out already. It was because one shoe would come on before the other one had got there … It was down to the individual adjustment of each lever, and that should have been engineered out'. In addition, the brake could never achieve optimum performance because the cam levers themselves were too short. It could work well enough, but the price was continual adjustment of the two levers' click-stop mechanisms, via awkward-to-use holes behind rubber plugs in the back of the hub. The previous brake had been superior in every way. The 7in rear brake was sls, no longer featuring fully floating shoes, and unexceptional; the big loss there was the optional qd facility for the rear wheel, which made puncture time a real pain.

The new shorty mudguards were impractical in the extreme and needed mudflaps if anything but dry miles were intended. The front one was hung on wire mountings which not only fractured from vibration but also eliminated the fork-brace effect of the previous substantial set of stays. This meant that with the braking forces acting on the right fork leg, the leg could fail to rebound until the brake was released, causing some interesting pogo action on corners. In mid-season, the original front stays were supplemented by an extra vertical

wire stay. Above the forks, the flat-back headlamp was also supported on fracture-prone wire, and it carried no ammeter, which had been a useful fitment. It did however revert to a circular light switch far less easy for the rider to reach out and use than the previous toggle switch had been. The flat shell carried on its back three warning lights – oil pressure, main beam and now an amber one for the new Lucas direction indicators – but given the lamp's flat back, unlike their predecessors, the lights often proved hard to make out in sunlight, and were later given hoods to help visibility.

The winkers themselves were erratic in the extreme, and the new Lucas alloy switch gear (the control levers were also alloy), was awkward, unreliable and not waterproof, and universally reviled. The petrol tank had lost its knee grips and paint suffered accordingly. There were other electrical backward steps, with the four-position ignition key returned to an awkward location in the side panel, the right-hand one this time; and behind that panel was also consigned the Zener diode, once more out of the cooling air. The two-part panels with their dummy louvres were difficult to

A short seat, desperate winkers, hideous 'gargoyle' tail-lamp housing – not everything changes for the better.

remove if you wanted to work on the carbs or get at the rectangular felt and wire mesh filters they contained. The only space for a toolkit was on top of the rear mudguard, under the hinged seat with its flimsy ammunition box style catch, and still with no lock. To check the battery level you now had to lift it out carefully from above, hoping the wires were long enough and wouldn't snag or pull off as you did so; a contrast with the previous practical access via the left-side panel. The coils, (previously out of the way under the tank), the rectifier and a capacitor were also crammed under the seat. The X-slotted oil filler cap was awkward to undo, to replace and to fill, and once you had undone it, the dipstick was no longer integral with the cap; it was now a separate metal rod with a looped end, hung on a bar just below the cap, where careless or oily fingers could quite easily drop it into the depths of the oil-bearing tube …

The wonderful Windtone horns had been replaced by the previous single one, and last of all, the teat-type tail-light assembly, which US legislation required should protrude beyond the back of the machine, was now housed on a hideous elongated mounting which the Yanks called the 'gargoyle'. So it would be fair to say that the new T120 was scarcely an improvement on the old one. Despite its merits,

this Bonneville had lost its go-anywhere versatility and become primarily a short-haul blaster. As Bob Currie put it, 'whatever it was, the rehashed [o-i-f] bike just wasn't the Bonnie as we'd known it.'

The engine, as mentioned, featured modified rocker boxes, which involved new rocker covers, studs, bolts and gaskets. This set-up had new access plugs on each side of the rocker boxes, to facilitate setting the valve clearances, although this remained a fiddly job. The rocker boxes had to be milled internally to give the necessary clearance for assembly, and they were then fitted with the help of four locating dowels. Two-stage bolts were now used to attach the rocker boxes to the cylinder head, with the lower section Allen-keyed and torqued down on the cylinder, while the upper stage secured the rocker boxes by threading into the lower part. Unfortunately it was found that over-tightening of the new rocker box bolts could loosen the main cylinder head studs.

The pushrod tubes were redesigned yet again. The oil-pressure relief valve became a single (UNF) assembly, and at the bottom end, the engine sprocket's oil seal face was removed and a modified distance piece fitted, so shims could be used to tackle the perennial problem of rapid wear from misalignment of the duplex primary chain. At the heart of the motor, the flywheel was modified once again, which entailed new bolts and flat washers. Overall, the gearing was lowered a little in line with US tastes for a rousing standing quarter, by the use of a 47 rather than the previous 46-tooth rear sprocket. Claimed power was increased to 50bhp at 7,000rpm. In mid-year, the clutch shock absorber front and plates changed to a through-bolt design.

Then shortly after that, fate struck this ill-starred machine with a final affliction. From GE 27029, as a result of a worldwide bearing shortage, the timing side crankcase and the

The author having a blast on a 1971 Bonnie (in Tiger colours). Most enjoyable, in fact.

crankshaft itself were altered to fit a metric timing side ball main bearing. This led to an epidemic of main bearing failures, according to John Nelson affecting as many as one in three machines in the 1971–2 period, with the continuing bearing shortage making replacements hard to find.

This came at a time when Meriden could ill afford the additional warranty expense. For by the end of 1971, the BSA Group was in debt to the tune of no less than £22 million. Jofeh left, and Lord Shawcross took over as a caretaker head for the Group. The struggle to survive entailed the decision to run Small Heath down and bring the BSA marque to an end. Lack of cash would dictate the minimal development work undertaken on the Triumph twins from then on.

For its young ridership however, the restyled Bonnie did not seem so bad, and both the new and rebellious *Bike* magazine in the UK, and *Cycle Guide* in the States, liked it. The latter found the finish excellent and the handling precise, while Mark Williams of *Bike* found (despite the dual seat being shorter than previously), that the T120 was good two-up. It had a grab-rail fitted which was a new version of the old design, but now carrying the reflectors, and all in chrome. He enjoyed its effortless power and ability to cruise at a steady 85mph (137kph). *Cycle Guide* found the bike vibrated only mildly, although a *Motor Cycle Sport* test spoke of vibration between 4,000 and 5,000rpm, but not as a major issue; 0 to 60 times of under 6 seconds were more on their mind! None of the tests mention oil leaks either.

Since April 1971 for the US, an optional five-speed gearbox was offered, based on the one developed for racing by Rod Quaife. Machines so equipped were designated T120RV and carried a 'Quaife 5-speed' sticker on the outer gearbox cover. (Later versions of the sticker in 1972 went first on the tail-light housing, and

then in 1973, on the rear mudguard.) These boxes fitted a roller race for the sleeve gear. In the clutch mechanism, a new three-ball clutch lever was used to counter lost movement. The five-speed box may not have been as trendy as an electric start or a disc brake, or even strictly necessary, but in this area at least, it brought the Bonnie into line with the Oriental opposition. Unfortunately, according to Brooke and Gaylin, early variants in the US arrived with their layshaft first and second gears and their drive dogs not carburized (oil-bath cooled), and they broke under moderate-to-heavy use. A US dealer recalled that 'our warranty claims as a result of those five-speeds were just enormous', with over 1,000 machines requiring repair. Once functioning, they were effective

enough, with a T120RV recording a 13.9
standing quarter on test with *Cycle World*, who
headlined 'A Five-Speed Transmission Makes
the Difference'. ('. . . you don't need a five-
speed gearbox to enjoy the Triumph
Bonneville. But it sure is neat.') They found it
eliminated some of the inertial problems of the
old box, making for quicker, smoother
changes, although they, like the UK test in
Motor Cycle, still considered its unchanged top
gear to be on the low side.

Despite the o-i-f's troubles, Meriden
nevertheless was producing more machines
than ever – according to Gaylin, more than
30,000 twins were built for 1971–2 – as Hele
and Hopwood struggled to reverse
Umberslade's impracticalities. Despite the new
T120R's initial chopper image, the US slice of
the market for Triumphs was in fact no longer
quite so predominant. Even in 1970's peak
export profit year, of the £10 million total which
BSA/Triumph had earned, just £2.75 million
had emanated from the USA. Business with
Europe had expanded, other markets had been
developed worldwide, and a UK boom for the
1970s was coming after the '60s slump. Many
of these markets required more practical (and
waterproof) features than the US-orientated '71
'choppers' carried. So, in the mid-season of
1971, a slab-sided petrol tank holding a more

realistic 4 (Imp) gallons was offered, styled a bit
like the one on contemporary Laverdas but
without the flair. It was also always to be
essential that the bracing bar, or 'panting strip',
as they were known at Meriden, should be
bolted on under the nose to join this tank's two
halves, or vibration could soon split them. The
big tank's sides were finished in Tiger Gold
surrounded in black which narrowed to a 4in
(100mm) black strip on the tank top. These
early versions came with a cheap-looking
Triumph name sticker in black and silver. For
1972, UK machines so equipped came with
traditional 'pull back' handlebars.

Engine changes for **1972** included new con
rod cap nuts and big ends. From CG50464 the
oil pressure release valve changed back to a
two-part assembly, and full-width timing gears
with two holes for an extractor were fitted. From
XG42304 came a more major change, a
redesigned cylinder head which saw an end to
those spontaneously detaching rocker
inspection caps. The four caps were replaced
by a pair of flat-finned covers bolted on fore
and aft. The head also featured bolted-on inlet
manifolds to replace the previous screwed-in
stubs, and eliminated the steel screwed-in
stubs for the exhaust; the linked pipes were
now just a push-fit into the head, from which,
unfortunately, they would prove all too ready to
pop out again. The new head retained a
revised version of the two-stage attachment
through-bolts, and featured four new internal
holding-down bolts.

The electrics saw the switch-gear layout
revised, but the switches stayed as vulnerable
and user unfriendly as before. The winker
stems became the same as fitted to the Trident,
with shorter ones at the front, and a slightly
louder version of the Lucas 6H horn was fitted.
From CG 50414 a new coil mounting plate
under the dual seat incorporated a (cramped)
tool shelf.

The 1972 models sported knee grips again on the big, 4-gallon tank, which was now finished with a Tiger Gold upper and a black-lined lower Cold White stripe. The smaller 3.5 (US) gallon tanks in Tiger Gold were finished with either a single set of swept wings in black-lined Cold White running back from the upper corners of the tank badges, or a full set of upper and lower scallops as in 1969–70. The mudguards for all were again Tiger Gold, including the stays, with a black-lined white centre stripe. Late in the model year, for the US, a version of the old 'slimline' 2.5 (US) gallon tank was offered; these versions lacked the previous raised centre seam, and were sent to

The 1972 T120 was halfway sensible, with a 4-gallon tank.

US dealers unpainted. Other finish details included black brake-plates for some UK models, and black-painted 'gargoyle' tail-lamp mounts for some US ones.

For 1972, in April, after two interim versions of the frame (uncatalogued, so as not to compromise unsold stocks of the existing tall ones), a final Series C chassis brought the seat height down to a true 31in (790mm) again. This was done by a combination of shorter fork springs, a seat with less comfortable, thinner padding, now hinged from further back, and later with a narrower nose, plus shorter (12.3in/312mm) rear units. These measures had been applied to stocks of the existing frame. But now the main change involved lowering the rear sub-frame some 3in (75mm),

The 1973 T140, a sanitised twin, with disc front brake, proper mudguards, fork gaiters, a new seat and tank motif. These silencers were for this year only.

at the point where its tubes were welded on to the main oil-bearing spine. All this meant new side panels, air filter assemblies and battery fittings, as well as a slightly revised rear mudguard. There was a new cross-brace under the seat, and at the same time, the 'ammunition box' seat clip changed to a plunger catch. As Gaylin points out, apart from the rear wheel and swinging arm, 'virtually every other item cannot be interchanged with the earlier machines'. While effective, the frame revision also carried a penalty. The point where the sub-frame joined would remain a potential fracture spot, especially for machines like police bikes which carried extra weight at the rear. Testers in 1972, however, found that the lowered frame cornered even better. This was just as well, because apart from a swinging-arm pivot strengthened later by extending the rear guard mounting plates to the main frame tube, this was the frame that would take Meriden's Bonneville to the end of its road.

A final decisive factor in the new Bonneville's fortunes and its place in the motorcycling world, and one somewhat obscured by the passage of time, was price. This was already a period of rampant inflation, but in the UK the jump from £420 for 1970's T120, to £616 for an o-i-f T120R in Autumn 1971 was a defining moment, especially when a 750 Norton Commando could be had that year for £462. In the USA the rise was cushioned somewhat, from $1,440 in 1970 to $1,595 for 1972, but during that year the move to the five-gear T120RV bumped it up to $1,725, which was then the price of a small car. In the UK, between 1970 and 1980, the price of a Bonneville exactly quadrupled, ending at £1,699! Edward Turner's great achievement with his twins had been to provide affordable performance for all riders, but from

now on the love of Triumph would prove an increasingly expensive emotion. This further eroded the marque's popular base, at the same time as the twin's performance was being leap-frogged by a new generation of superbikes.

Meriden's cleaning up process for the twins was just about completed in **1973**. Longer, more effective mudguards were fitted, in chrome, with chromed versions of the three 1970-type mudguard stays. The old bullet-shaped chromed headlamp shell was back, carrying the easy-to-use three-position toggle light switch, and mounted on properly substantial black-painted 'ears', which were rubber-mounted and detachable. The front forks, which as we shall see were new, had polished alloy sliders, and on UK versions wore clipless gaiters to help protect the oil seals; the left hand fork top now also carried the ignition switch. The silly louvred side panels were revised to a single but two-part plastic moulded panel on each side, each bearing a long rectangular nameplate with a chrome surround, in place of previous transfers. New longer, quieter silencers, with rounded ends for that year only, suited the UK tank bike's overall look. At the rear, the 'gargoyle' gave place to a chunkier polished alloy tail-light mounting for a new, squared-off Lucas L917 tail-lamp, with the rear set of winkers moved forward on to the grab-rail/lifting handle. The 4-gallon tank gained a nice looking 'comma' paint design and a proper metal 'Triumph' tank badge. The tank was matched by a new seat, with chrome base trim, uptilted at the rear and easier on both the eye and the posterior.

This UK spec Bonnie was a chunky, functional looking machine, and the US version was back on flamboyant form too, with the UK improvements, but also naked forks with chromed top covers and headlamp supports, quite extreme 8in (200mm)-rise handlebars, the previous megaphone-style silencers and the 'slimline' tank bearing the 'picture-frame' badge. Both versions also came with two major new developments.

The first was a front disc brake, pretty well mandatory on modern machines since 1969. The 10in (250mm) chrome-plated Lockheed disc was mounted on the left, with the caliper rear of the fork, as Norton and Trident experience had proved this was best. The master cylinder sat on handlebars which in both UK and US form had been revised to accommodate it, and whose handlebar levers had changed from alloy to chromed steel. The caliper carried a chrome cover with a circular 'Triumph Hydraulic' sticker. The brake was an undoubted improvement over what had come before it, although it would suffer from a rather 'wooden' feel, and performed poorly in the wet. Another problem was the chrome wearing off the disc and chewing up the pads, which when it happened, reduced pad life to 2,000 miles or less. Many owners preferred to pre-empt this, by skimming the disc back to its basic iron. In 1973, later in the year, the rear brake cam and its liner were also revised.

The new disc, as mentioned, sat between new forks, largely derived from those on the T150V Trident. This meant new top and bottom yokes; the top yokes carried extra slots allowing the stanchion top spigots to be clamped by hexagon-headed cap screws. Sliders and stanchions were interchangeable with the '73 disc-braked T150V and as on the triples, the left fork leg now had an integral cast lug for the caliper. Internally new springs were fitted, but the damper tubes and valve assemblies were unchanged.

For the Bonnie, to match this modern brake, 1973 also saw the move, long-awaited in America, to a 750cc capacity.

This process was troubled (see '750 Twins'), and the troubles would continue. Most of these stemmed from the fact that financial constraints had meant that the T140V was basically a 750 top end on the 650's bottom. Hele's engineer on the conversion, John Barton, told how 'our original (750 Bonnevilles) would do over 120mph (190kph), but we had to detune them because the crank was so weak – it had been designed for the 650.' The detuning consisted of compression reduced for UK bikes to 7.9:1 (although 8.6:1 remained standard for the US), and camshafts switched from the T120's race-bred profiles to a soft 1950s' touring profile with 1⅛in radius tappets for the T140's exhaust cam, although the sportier Spitfire profile with ¾in radius tappets went on the inlet. Figures for bhp were no longer readily available, although 52bhp at 6,200rpm was subsequently claimed. The depressing fact was that the production T140 was actually slightly slower at the top end than the best T120s, although it did possess good grunt and mid-range power. But it was also thirstier – 650 Bonnevilles habitually returned 55–60mpg overall, but the T140V gave in the region of 45–55mpg – and this was significant, in the years of the 1970s' Middle East oil crisis. The T140V in 1973 was also more expensive at £649, but the remaining 650s matched its price rise.

The new 750 engines featured a 10-stud cylinder head, with the extra one a second holding-down stud in the space between the rocker boxes. According to Norman Hyde, this was to help counter gas leakage at the head gasket in the reduced area between the enlarged bores. For the same reason, bolts of high expansion metal were introduced to reduce likely distortion of the head castings. There were also new locating dowels between the head and rocker box to stop shuffling and protect the gaskets. The T140V came with a solid copper head gasket, and Hyde said this contributed to continuing problems with blown gaskets, until a composite one was fitted in 1978. The new head also featured cast aluminium adapters for the splayed inlet port, and a new manifold balance pipe. The cylinder block was shorter and stiffer, and inside it, ⅛in shorter, heavier section con rods were fitted. Oil circulation was improved by enlarging the size of the block's internal oilways and increasing the oil pump capacity.

The 750's timing side main bearing became heavier duty, and the crankshaft, although carrying the previous flywheel, was revised, with new bolts and a balance factor of 74 per

The new 750 engine with revised rocker inspection plates.

Meriden workers in October 1973 begin a long picket.

cent. On its drive-side end, the primary chain was increased to a triplex item, which while stronger, continued to experience problems of alignment and wear. Gearing was raised slightly, with a 20-tooth gearbox sprocket replacing the 19-tooth one. There was a redesigned clutch shock absorber spider, and clutch springs 30 per cent stronger could make clutch operation a Charles Atlas exercise for several years to come.

Many were disappointed with the T140. 'Somewhere along the line it seems to have lost its magic,' a *Motor Cycle* test recorded after struggling to reach 100mph. They appreciated the new brake, the engine's flexibility and the bike's lightness, but not the vibration. Another seasoned tester, Vic Willoughby, would judge that in his experience 'only one (motorcycle) vibrated worse than the big Triumph … the 500 Triumph GP racer.' But not everyone agreed; *Cycle World* called the T140V 'the best Bonneville to date'. It certainly still handled, stopped and sounded right.

For 1973, the T140V 750s were offered in conjunction with 650 variants, with the UK 650s

used as a way of disposing of remaining high-seat frames, although by the end of the model year they too featured the revised chassis and five-speed gearbox. Finish on the 1973 US T140V models saw the 'slimline' tank adopt a single pair of gold 'scallops' with a modified shape starting out from the top of the tank badge, while the hole for the single fixing bolt was covered by a black rubber grommet and a white plastic badge bearing a raised 'Triumph' logo in gold. Colours for the UK T120s continued in 1972's Tiger Gold and black-lined Astral White, mudguards included. The T140s carried the chromed mudguards, and their tank colours were a deep tangerine shade called Hi-Fi Vermilion, and white-lined Gold for the 'comma' design on their sides.

But during 1973, events within and outside the ailing Group were conspiring to nearly sweep away both models. Already the US dealer network had been shaken and depleted by the offering of Triumph franchises to previous BSA dealers, and those that remained were subject to several new managements, and were also faced with shortages of 650

750 Twins

In keeping with the urge of typical Bonnie owners to buy the quickest bike available and then make it go even faster, 750cc conversions had been available for the T120 on both sides of the Atlantic for some time. In the UK, good big bore kits could be had from ARE and Morgo, as well as the 686cc hop-up from Weslake with its eight-breathing 750 head, which would later form the basis of one of the last Bonneville variants, the TSS in 1982. Percy Tait had raced a Meriden Experimental 750 twin in 1968, before the Trident took over. In the US, big bore conversions from several sources had long been available, and one of the best of these was Sunny Routt's Webcor kit.

In 1969, there was a relaxation of the Harley-friendly AMA rule which had restricted OHV machines in Class C (Roadster-based) competition to a capacity of 500cc, a rule which had given Milwaukee's fire-breathing 750 side-valves a useful edge on the mile and half-mile dirt tracks. OHV 750s were now eligible, and TriCor's Rod Coates wanted to take advantage of this with a homologated 750 Triumph twin. The result was the slightly dodgy T120RT, a model which contrary to regulations, was not produced at Meriden, but consisted of a batch of 200 1970 T120s, which were then covertly kitted out at Baltimore and Duarte with Routt 3in bore (recorded as 76mm) cast iron barrels, plus 10.5:1 forged pistons to match. For the benefit of the AMA inspectors, these barrels had then been doctored to resemble Meriden cylinders. They had radiused corners machined on the cylinder base flange, although those responsible missed the maker's logo, a triangle containing the initials of the cylinder's manufacturer – Motor Castings – but luckily the AMA inspectors missed this too. It appears that 204 of these 750s were built in all, and Gene 'Burrito' Romero rode a T120RT to victory in that year's AMA Grand National Championships.

This naturally increased Stateside demand for a 750 roadster to fever pitch, and there was reason enough – the Commando, CB750, XLCH Harley and soon Yamaha, were all conspiring to make 650 look like yesterday's man. But Hele and Hopwood stubbornly resisted. From experience, taking BSA and Norton twins out to 750, they knew the problems involved, including increased vibration, and Hopwood also knew that higher output US dirt-track twins were cracking their cranks on a regular basis. They wanted a Triumph 750 twin to be an all-new development, such as Hele's short-stroke balanced design. But as the Group crashed, money ran out and pressure to shift unsold 650s in the US mounted, Hopwood, according to BSACI's Pete Colman, finally succumbed to his pressure.

Even so, Hopwood halted the 750's intended release earlier in 1972, and when the converted 650 did appear in September for the '73 season, it was in two stages. According to Experimental man Norman Hyde, this was due to the original drawings having been done with barrel castings bored out, but with no increase in their wall thickness. These could safely be taken to the required 76mm – but no further ie there was no provision for a rebore. So, from September 1972/JH15435, the '750' came in a cautious interim form with a 75mm bore, which in conjunction with the 650's 82mm stroke, gave a true 724cc. Only in December, from XH22018, did new cylinder castings become available, permitting the final (76 x 82mm) 744cc dimensions.

On the T120RT, the Motor Castings' 'MC' logo was the only giveaway on Triumph's first official 750.

The T140 engine.

The T140 Bonneville for 1974.

spares, which would deepen catastrophically in the following years. Meanwhile in the UK, the Tory government's Department of Trade and Industry was persuaded that the way forward for the ailing motorcycle industry lay in a merger of what remained of the BSA/Triumph Group, with Dennis Poore's lower volume but superficially successful Norton Villiers concern, who by then were making only Commandos. After a Stock Exchange fracas in March 1973, BSA shares plummeted, and the merger

became a virtual take-over by Poore.

Naturally this intensified anxiety at Meriden, and this time it was justified. Hele and Hopwood met Poore, to find that, in Hopwood's words, 'the detailed strategy we had worked out so enthusiastically for the past 12 months was thrown out forthwith as far too ambitious.' Out went H and H's proposed modular range; Hopwood left, while Hele stayed with the core of Experimental for the next two under-funded years working for the

new Norton Villiers Triumph
(NVT) concern, until that too
foundered. Poore had a 'master
plan' which involved selling the
Meriden site to Jaguar and continuing
motorcycle production at Small Heath and
Wolverhampton, where Commandos were then

The final UK T120 650, in handsome Purple and Cold White.

produced. When this was put to the Meriden workforce during September 1973, under the direction of union officials and local Labour MPs, they imposed an immediate partial blockade, the beginning of nearly two years of industrial strife, which effectively halted production. It ended with the establishment, with the blessing of the new Labour government's Minister, Tony Benn, of the Meriden Workers Co-operative.

The **1974** model year had therefore been

terminated abruptly, but some developments had taken place and they were incorporated into machines blockaded in the factory. During a lull in hostilities several hundred of these, the majority of around 300 being 650s, were released for sale, from engine numbers JJ58080 to NJ60032, and then a few more were sold when co-op production commenced, to engine number NJ60083.

In the '74 engine the rocker boxes had been revised to counter oil leaks, and now featured

two extra cover fixing screws, and improved gaskets. On the top of the primary chaincase, the junction for the large bore breather pipe became black plastic. The oil pressure relief valve fitted a finer mesh filter gauze, and a new oil pressure indicator switch with an extended rubber cover was introduced. The gearbox final drive sprocket was altered to take a new sprocket nut lock-washer and O-ring oil seal. The front mudguard mountings were strengthened and attached to a thicker

mounting bracket on the fork leg. And on UK models, the silencers became their final long 'cigar' form with near-parallel tail sections, a little more restrictive on performance but civilised, yet still giving a soul-stirring throaty roar. Colours were deployed as for 1973, but became the very attractive Cherokee Red and gold-lined White for the T140V, and the stunning purple and gold-lined Cold White for the T120V, which now had the chromed mudguards.

1976 to 1978: Days of hope

The co-op began with some exhilaration on the part of people who took pride in their product and tradition, and who after a long struggle seemed temporarily in control of their own destiny. A small number of seasoned engineers, men like John Nelson, Alex Scobie, Harry Woolridge and Brian Jones, returned over the years to Meriden and would do their best to make this traditional machine as good as it could be, while also keeping up with the changing requirements of both noise and emission legislation, and fashion. There could be no question of keeping up with the Japanese, but as just about the sole survivor of the British industry, the Bonnie undeniably retained a potential niche market. Its appeal was summed up in the word 'character'. Unfortunately, the bottom line was that the final settlement of the industrial dispute had left Meriden permanently under funded, and they would remain in that restrictive condition until the end. Production standards were inevitably uneven.

The **1976** Bonnevilles can be taken as starting at HN62501 in July 1975, as this was the first production T140V with the left-foot gear change required by US legislation, as well as by NVT, who at that stage were (with great reluctance) marketing the co-op's product. This model also featured the first rear disc brake. The left-side shift for years made these T140s a 'no-no' for stubbornly conservative (and nervous) British riders, the author included.

The change was carried out by running a simple steel rod, cranked to provide clearance round the clutch, from the gear pedal, which was shortened, to the back of the gearbox. This involved revised inner and outer gearbox covers and joint washers, and a suitable spindle bush, operating quadrant and kick-start axle. The primary cover too was modified, losing its rotor inspection plate, which was replaced by a screw-in plate with cross-slots. A revised handlebar clutch-operating mechanism went with the new gearchange, and for a while clutch cables became short-life items. The new mechanism worked well enough, although the change would be notchier than previously. The problem it threw up was in another area. The new pedal meant that the right and left footrests could now be standardised rather than handed as previously, but the position the rests had to adopt for the revised controls was too far forward. This restricted riding at speed, and also threw the rider's weight rearwards, so that running for more than an hour or so became uncomfortable – a pity, in a machine whose niche from then on should have been touring, as well as just short blasts down to the pub.

The rear disc brake featured a 0.235in thick 10in disc, and the front brake's disc was

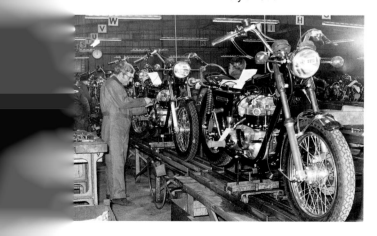

Meriden gets back to work, building 750 Bonnevilles, in late 1975.

increased to this thickness for standardisation. Although the caliper was underslung, the new brake meant that rear wheel removal remained difficult. The rear mudguard, swinging-arm and rear frame were modified to accommodate it, and attached to the latter, the pillion footrests were now mounted at a 45° rearward-facing angle to comply with US legislation, for the co-op was still pinning large hopes on the traditionally profitable North American market.

The brake's master cylinder was positioned under the seat, and the battery mounting, coil platform and tool tray had to be modified to suit. The right-side brake pedal pivoted on a modified right engine plate, and its control arm was repositioned so as to work the master cylinder. The new pedal was positioned fairly close in and with too long a reach from the rider's foot. The rear brake worked well in the dry, but like the front, not well in the wet, and its disc, also like the front, shed chrome and chewed up pads. In addition, its increased power could cause the 10-gauge wheel spokes to work loose and in the end to snap. Like the front wheel, the rear one with its new wheel spool, ran on unprotected wheel bearings which regularly failed at low mileages.

There were other changes to the co-op's first offering. Once again it was US legislation which was the spur for the Lucas handlebar switchgear to be labelled. The thumb-switches themselves became longer and easier to use, and on the left the labelling was cast-in; but on the right, functions were indicated by tacky transparent transfers, which naturally did not often stand the test of time. On the headlamp

The 'Cider Slider'. In Summer 1977, Meriden and Bulmer's Strongbow Cider collaborated to build a team of Gordon Matthews-framed 750s and launch US-style dirt-track racing in England. Sadly, this came to nothing.

also, black stickers with silver lettering were attached for the switch and warning lights, with another on the left side headlamp mounting ear, above the ignition switch housing. New petrol caps with 'On/Off' and 'Reserve' markings were also fitted, but these had plastic internals, wore rapidly and then leaked. The faces of the Smith's instruments lost their previous NVT 'wiggly worm' logo.

The oil pressure relief valve was fitted with an O-ring seal, and the oil pump junction block, feed and return pipes were revised. The cigar-shaped silencers fitted redesigned internals for extra quietness, with the modified versions identifiable by their concave dished end-plates, and the right-hand silencer's hanger was altered to allow for the brake hose. Induction noise was addressed by intake silencer tubes fitted to the filter elements, and their plastic covers bolted from the outside. The Amal Concentric carburettors were now Spanish-made and carried extended tickler buttons. The throttle cable became a single one with a twist grip to suit and a junction box further down its length. Another new dual seat was fitted with thickened padding and a new black vinyl cover, still with the aerated, cross-ribbed top, but now with black piping along the top edge, and the bottom chrome trim featuring black rubber borders; the seat pan was also changed to permit both hinges to be the same. In mid-year, the front mudguard mountings changed to a single T160 Trident-style chromed rear wraparound stay, in combination with a strong central bridge. The mudguard itself was not drilled for a front number plate as these 'pedestrian slicers' were no longer a legal requirement in the UK.

For both the UK and US T140V twins, the 1975 tank finish was as announced for the UK models in 1974, ie Cherokee Red and gold-lined Cold White, and arranged in the same way (UK 'comma', US top 'scallops'). For 1976

The Jubilee Bonneville

The UK T140J Silver Jubilee cut a dash in patriotic colours.

One of the workers' unpaid advisors was the former Chairman of British Leyland, Lord Stokes, and one of his ideas was to capitalise on the fact that 1977 was the year of the Queen's Silver Jubilee. The Bonneville was therefore offered in T140J (for Jubilee) guise. The Palace approved this limited edition model, which came with a commemorative certificate in both UK and US versions, as did the special finish. The T140J's mudguards, tank, side panels and rear chainguard were finished in an appropriate but undistinguished silver. The mudguards carried a blue centre stripe lined with outer white and inner red. The chromed wheel rim centres were striped similarly. The T140 Jubilee's tyres were Dunlop K91s with a thin red stripe and a red direction arrow on their side walls. The rear chainguard bore a curved blue flash tapering to a point at its rear, again lined with white outer and red inner stripes. The tank 'commas' or 'scallops' were in blue, with double white lining sandwiching a middle red line in both cases.

The T140J's engine covers were also chrome-plated, as was the tail-light housing, where for the stock '77 T140s this had been painted black, rather than its previous polished alloy finish. All Jubilees also sported the US T140's chromed top fork covers. The Jubilee's most unusual styling feature was its seat, which was all-blue with red piping, and 'Triumph Silver Jubilee' stencilled on the back in silver. The seat cover changed to a style which would be adopted for the whole range the following year; a non-aerated top with a narrower cross-hatched section, the piping swooping down to define the sides of the rider's portion. Another feature soon to be gained by all was the Girling shock-absorbers, which were 'upside-down' (ie with the pre-load adjusters uppermost); they provided a stable but rather harsh ride. A final soon-for-all innovation was the side panels, which were now one piece, going over the top of the previous covers, secured by a single screw each, with the help of a tension spring fastening them together at the front. On the Jubilee these panels came with special emblems, with a chopped off triangular portion below the standard name badge bearing the Union Jack and the words 'One of a Thousand', or after an extra 400 had been built, 'Limited Edition'.

Originally, numbers were to have been limited to 1,000 of each variant, but overseas demand meant an additional 400 or so were produced, many buyers storing them as investments.

Gaylin points out that the US version sold very slowly, as Americans could not identify with the Royal event and found the finish over-the-top, but the model did well for Meriden. Despite being £150 dearer than that year's stock T140, as Brian Jones put it, 'it may have been just cosmetic but we sold the lot, and 50 per cent of the owners put them away and never ran them – that's the way – the warranty call-back was minimal!'

The 1977 UK Jubilee T140 made a good stab at handsome romanticism.

The first side panel (left) was before Meriden decided to make the Jubilee a slightly less limited edition (right).

Even the seat cover of the Jubilee was customised. (Shame about the colour.)

Many Jubilees, like this one at the London Motorcycle Museum, were salted away as investments.

the main colour changed to gold-lined Polychromatic Red. Although a small quantity of US specification machines had been offered in the UK both just before and during the sit-in, from now on the US T140s, with their naked front forks, peanut tanks and 8in high bars, would be fully available in Blighty, and they were popular, outselling the sensible UK variants from then on.

The Bonnie would become something of a cult bike and this was as well, for the price of the first co-op bikes had risen to £837 and would continue to rise from then on. The T140s suffered from their hot running, riding position, lack of electric start and vibration. (A *Bike* magazine test late in 1975 suffered three blown fuses, a loosened left winker arm and winkers going berserk at speed – all about par for the course – as well as finding the continuous vibration at 80mph numbing.) This had to be balanced against the great mid-range power ('amazing torque' – *Bike*); the generally excellent handling, limited only by a left centre-stand extension which had at least one journo off; lightness, with a catalogued dry weight of 390lb (177kg) (when modern big bikes were at least 100lb/45kg heavier), classic-enough good looks, especially with the 'slimline' tank; and finally, the lure, somewhere between glamour and patriotism, of the Triumph name.

These machines were not yet reliable, with their vulnerable wheel bearings, short-wear shock absorbers and above all, still-unreliable electrics – both a 1980 *Cycle World* T140 owner's survey and another in *Superbike* in 1986, identified electrics as the prime cause of discontent, with shorts in a wiring harness too full of bullet connectors, the vulnerable switches including the ignition/light switch, and contact breakers still prone to getting out of adjustment. But at least the latter problem would be solved soon, and spares, when they could be had again, were cheap, and available, which was not the case with many Japanese machines. Also, the charismatic gutsy twins were no more unreliable, or expensive, than 1970s Harley-Davidsons!

Little or no technical changes occurred in **1977** as the co-op concentrated on production and surviving – some 20,000 machines being built in 1976 and 1977.

All 1977 T140s had modified front mudguards with the central braces altered to a flat bridge supporting the guard from underneath and a tongue projecting ahead to brace the forward section, secured by a screw from above. This revised arrangement would lead to a resurgence of mudguard splitting. The UK bikes also came with metal electrical suppressor spark plug caps, which proved vulnerable to rain.

Standard T140s that year for the first time came in a choice of colours, a ploy thereafter increasingly resorted to by Meriden, given the absence of cash for significant development or new models. The previous year's Polychromatic Red and Cold White were supplemented by an optional Polychromatic Blue (known as Pacific Blue in the US), and gold-lined Cold White.

It was a hinge year for the co-op in 1978. Production reached a peak at one short of 12,000, and the year saw a major technical innovation, with both the volume and the redesign being primarily aimed at the USA. But a weak dollar meant that with machine prices for US distributors already fixed, Meriden's hoped-for profits were wiped out, and turned into a £700,000 loss. This was the start of a continuous financial decline until the end, as well as the finish of the US market for Triumph, which from then on would only take around 1,000 machines a year.

The **1978** T140Vs embodied some substantial problem-solving. With compression standardised at 7.9:1 for all markets, they began by replacing the troublesome solid copper head gasket with a more effective 'eyeletted composition' one. The front forks also fitted new, self-aligning oil seals and retainers, so oil tightness was somewhat improved all round. The upside-down Gas Girlings went on UK models from the start, and US ones from mid-year. Sealed wheel bearings were finally in place at both ends, and in the rear wheel, stronger 9-gauge spokes were fitted. The 6H horn was revised again, a new headlamp unit incorporating a Halogen main bulb was fitted, and from mid-year, good Yuasa batteries replaced the Lucas ones. Other detail changes included fitting a locking washer in place of the previous lock tab washer on the crankshaft rotor nut, and a gasket between the gearbox inner and outer covers. In mid-year an interrupted supply of Smith's instruments led to a progressive change-over to Swiss Veglia ones. UNF threads came in for the rockers and their adjuster screws, together with dot-and-dash timing marks on the cam wheels. Finally the new-style side panels and seat covers as on the Jubilee were introduced. But sadly the seat's padding was not substantial enough, and in either the broad- or narrow-nosed versions made to suit the UK and US tanks respectively, this seat again proved uncomfortable on long runs.

Bonnies were again offered in three alternative colour finishes in 1978, which ranged from the sublime to the ridiculous, namely for the US the very attractive, nay, definitive, black and gold-striped Candy Apple red, plus the equally nice Astral Blue and gold-lined Silver. Less appealing was Chocolate Brown with Gold, double-striped in white outer and brown inner. On these machines the side panels and seat cover were also colour co-ordinated in brown. No less than 480 of these unpopular brown US T140s had to be shipped

back to the UK, which wiped out the profits on their eventual sale. UK Bonnies with the brown finish, were called Tawny Brown, with the gold 'comma' lined in white outer and brown inner, and the brown seat covers; as well as an Aquamarine and Silver variant double-striped in black inner and gold outer. UK mudguards, for this year only, were painted in the machine's main colour, with U-shaped stripes halfway along them, pointing forward on the front, backward on the rear, and double-lined as were the tanks. The UK side panels were also painted in the machine's main colour, but with a hockey stick-shaped stripe in the second colour running along the bottom of the panel before angling up at the panel's rear until level with the middle of the name badge, the 'stick' being double-lined like the tank. The UK machines from now on were fitted the US chrome fork top covers, and in a final cosmetic touch for all, the tail-light housing reverted to polished alloy, now also lacquered.

A more substantial variation had been initiated by the USA's Environmental Protection Agency's directives on emissions for vehicles built from 1 January 1978. Brian Jones and Jock Copeland had designed a new cylinder head, with new type carburettors and revised

Any colour you like. This was the range of pigments for 1979 750 Triumphs.

The 1979 T140E 'American' – real Stateside exports did not wear gaiters.

engine breathing, to meet this legislation's requirements. On the head, the Bonnie's trademark splayed carburettors passed away in favour of parallel inlet ports. Integrally cast stubs, to take the new carburettors' rubber inlet collars, replaced the previous detachable inlet manifolds. Internally the combustion chamber was slightly reshaped and redesigned iron valve guides, plus new valve spring cups, were fitted.

The new Amal Concentric Mk 2 carbs featured square bodies and PTFE-coated alloy slides. The float tickler was gone, as this had been the means by which the Mk 1 had vented its float chamber to air, an emission which the EPA sought to eliminate. On the Mk 2, a cold-starting enrichment jet was controlled by a vertical slide valve, which was operated for both closely packed instruments by a single small lever, mounted on the left carburettor and checked by a click spring. This was a rather on/off arrangement which made progressive use of choke while warming up awkward, and the Mk2s would prove to not really suit the Bonneville, particularly in the mid-range. The new set-up was found to work best with Champion N5 plugs, but one cumulative result of the changes was petrol consumption

improved to a welcome 50 to 55mpg.

The new models fitted a modified version of the Jubilee-type side panels. These were joined by a second fixing spring which crossed over beneath the carburettors. The new, one-piece panels stuck out further than before beyond the seat nose and within them, the airbox housing was redesigned and used new connecting rubbers.

The big engine breather tube from the crankcase now went straight to the airbox, again to prevent venting to atmosphere, and for the same reason, the oil-in-frame's breather was linked to the exhaust rocker box. These models were designated T140E. The redesign was a necessary evil, but it did further limit the Bonneville's performance. A *Motor Cycle Mechanics* test of one of the new models in January 1979 noted a sudden drop off at the higher end of the rev range. On the dyno however, the engine produced a genuine 49.5bhp at 6,500rpm, and they still managed 110mph top speed, as did *Bike* magazine, although the strong point remained that lovely surging mid-range torque. As *MCM* concluded, all the power was stowed in the lower and middle range, where it could be used, in spite of vibration.

1979 to 1988: Last things

MCM's test bike was a **1979** machine, however, and that year had brought a substantial number of useful changes. First among these was the crankshaft, as Meriden put it, being 'machined differently' ie more comprehensively, and testers from then on, like *MCM*'s, often noted surprising smoothness, as well as oil-tight engines, on these final Bonnevilles. Another internal gain for 1979 was the replacement of the timing-side ball main bearing with an unusual SKF roller bearing, featuring a U-shaped outer cage with a top hat end piece which determined crankshaft end-float. In the gearbox the camplate was reprofiled to improve selection, and a neutral indicator switch was fitted. This activated (or sometimes, not) a neutral indicator light, which like the other warning lights, indicator signals and the ignition key, were now housed, and clearly labelled, in a T160 Trident-style instrument console located centrally between the Veglia speedo and tacho, both of which now had big rubber binnacles. In addition, the Lucas switchgear entered its final incarnation, with neat, integrally labelled switches in black housings. They were unchanged internally and still not waterproof, but were a big improvement and easier to use. The housings were extended to incorporate pivot bases for new alloy brake and clutch levers. These had been redesigned to give less of a stretch, as riders had been requesting for many years.

Elsewhere in the electrics, even greater gains were made by the fitting of Lucas Rita electronic ignition, a set-and-forget system impervious to vibration. The reluctor and pulse sensor were fitted in the old points' position on the timing chest, behind a smart new horizontally finned cover. The Rita's amplifier module went behind the right side panel. The other big step forward was the use of a Lucas RM24 three-phase alternator, whose greater output finally allowed continuous, worry-free use of daytime headlights, indicators etc. It came in conjunction with a new Lucas 3DS rectifier and an uprated Zener diode to take care of excess wattage. The new electrics involved a change, for the first time in three decades, from a positive to a negative earth system.

Externally the '79 T140Es were full of neat touches. All the engine case fasteners were now Allen-socket headed. There was, at last, a lock for the dual seat, as well as helmet locks on the upper right frame tube. Also fitted was a nice little chrome parcel rack with a weight limit of 15lb (6.8kg). For the UK, handlebars were narrowed by 2in (50mm) to 27in (686mm). New, squared-off footrest rubbers featured chamfered ends underneath for cornering at the maximum angle, although tests were still finding a lack of ground clearance at ultimate lean, due to both the centre-stand and footrests. The side panels were slightly revised and their indents reshaped to allow the fitting of a new two-level name badge, with the model name above and '750' below. The spooled wheel hubs were now lacquered as well as polished, front and rear.

All models reverted to chromed mudguards, and the finishes, with five coats of paint and the traditional hand-lining, were wonders to behold. The big tanks on the UK models lost their knee grips and swapped their 'comma' tank design for a diagonal zig-zag pattern with a flicked-down front end and a flicked-up back. UK side panels remained the same colour as the tank. The top UK colour was black with a Candy Apple Red tank panel lined with two gold stripes sandwiching a black one. There were also Astral Blue variants with Silver tank panels lined with two gold stripes sandwiching a blue one, and pale Gold tanks with deep metallic gold panels lined with a white outer and black inner stripe sandwiching a pale gold one. This model came with a brown seat cover. The US machines came with either a Candy Apple Red tank with double gold-lined 'scallops' and red side panels, or an Astral Blue and Silver version with blue side panels carrying name badges like the blue UK version, but with a special silver background. The third and most handsome

variant was Black with double gold-lined Silver 'scallops' and black side panels.

These machines were joined in March 1979 by the T140D Special. This was essentially a styling exercise triggered by Yamaha's successful XS650 Specials, but as with the Jubilee, it contained features which would soon become standard on the stock T140Es. The Specials were finished all in gold-lined black, with seven-spoke US Lester mag alloy wheels, and a carefully tuned two-into-one exhaust system. Unlike the UK versions of the Special, which failed to hit to spot aesthetically, the early US ones looked stunning.

The US exhaust system echoed the '65-on TT Specials. The pipes were finally, positively located in the head, clamped into spigots which were screwed into the exhaust ports. No balance tube connected the pipes, which angled in towards each other until they joined in front of the bottom of the downtubes, passing the latter beneath the frame on the right (so that a redesigned, better tucked-in centre stand could be retained). A similar Dunstall system was a favourite go-faster fitment for Triumph twins. The pipe then ran into a single silencer which was a new design of two-stage megaphone with an end-cap resembling the annular discharge T160 can. Although this silencer contributed to a 25lb (11kg) weight reduction and made wheel

removal easier and improved mid-range torque, it restricted top-end performance (T140Ds on test were pushed to top 100mph), and the exhaust system could still ground quite badly. This was ironic in view of the revised centre-stand and the fact that the footrests had been raised 2in (50mm) in pursuit of ground clearance; again, both these features would go on the whole range later. But to fit the silencer, the rear brake's caliper was mounted above the disc, a position less vulnerable to road spray, which would also soon be adopted by all models.

Another new feature was the Special's stepped, poorly proportioned, over-tall seat, which let it down in the styling stakes in pursuit of comfort. Unable to afford top quality foam throughout, the rider's portion at least was treated to 'cold cure' inserts beneath a new cross-hatched seat cover. Behind the seat came a revised rear mudguard support rail with a new squared-off grab rail, and no parcel rack. The front mudguard was a minimal item with no rear stay. To echo the black and alloy wheels, the 'points' cover had been painted black, with just the edges of its fins left in bare alloy.

A final worthwhile Special innovation taken up by all was a heavier section swinging arm. Nevertheless, the early Specials were prone to back-end weave. This has been attributed to an initial fat 4.25 x 18in rear tyre fitted for style purposes, which soon reverted to the then standard 4.10 x 18in cover, not only because of the handling problem, but also because the taller tyre had fouled the mudguard and caused some punctures.

The T140D's all-black US tank featured the metal Triumph badge, with thick gold-lined 'scalloped' outlines both above and below it. The side panels carried the new badges with Bonneville above and Special in red script below; beneath the badge there were two horizontal gold stripes. By 1980, UK versions of

The 1980 UK T140D Special sported a conventional exhaust system.

the T140D came with either the two-into-one or the stock twin exhaust system, and the black tank 'zig-zag' with thin outer and thick inner gold lines, sandwiching black.

With the US market gone, production in **1980** was down to a quarter of the previous year, and the co-op's manpower was sharply reduced in a painful blood-letting. But despite severe financial constrictions, still Meriden continued with useful improvements, and even a significant new model in mid-season. All T140s adopted the D Special's raised footrests and revised centre-stand, with the latter finally reinforced by additional braces to the frame tubes. The silencers were also tipped up at the back for better cornering. A slightly redesigned version of the stronger swinging arm, with diameter increased to 38mm from 32mm, was fitted, and the brake pedal strengthened. This necessitated a rerouted rear brake line with a

banjo union up by the rear caliper, which had moved above the disc, like the Ds. This in turn required the speedo drive to be relocated to the left of the wheel, resulting in a new hub, sprocket and disc bolts. The rear brake's fluid reservoir moved down to the master cylinder, and an access window was cut in the back portion of the right inner side cover, to comply with US safety regulations which required visual checking of the fluid level to be possible. For the same reason, on the handlebars the front brake master cylinder was now in white opaque plastic.

The Lucas indicator stalks were now rubber-mounted, although this was only partially effective. A larger tool-tray was fitted, and with check-stops now incorporated in the seat hinges, the previous check wire was abandoned. A long-standing service irritation for owners had been the excessively fiddly

The UK T140D demonstrates its big tank 1979-on 'zig-zag' motif.

method of primary chain adjustment, which had been guaranteed to have oil from the case running down your arm and on to the exhaust. The adjuster was now redesigned to prevent this happening.

A major innovation finally cured the previous vulnerability of the double-plunger oil pump suffering fatal damage from dirt. This was a new, four-valve pump incorporating secondary check ball-valves in both scavenge and feed circuits, requiring a modified pump body and hence timing cover.

The other big innovation was the fitting of an optional electric starter. Although this came a little late, and the motor selected was the Lucas M3, as previously used on the 1964 Norton Electra as well as for Reliant three-wheelers, and which by then was being manufactured under licence in India, Meriden made a better job of the conversion than their former Norton rivals had managed with their electric foot Commandos. It served a generation of riders who had never had to acquire the knack of kick-starting. From CB29901, batches of modified crankcases were produced, with the

starter motor being positioned behind the cylinder in the old magneto position. For these T140ES models, a new timing cover and inner crankcase extended to the rear to house the drive for the starter. This then worked in a reduction gear system through the timing gears, with a Borg-Warner sprag-type clutch driving on to a strengthened intermediate gear, which was firmly bushed on the timing cover and crankcase face. Reduction drive was set at a low 15:1, to ensure good cold-weather starting. The now not very shapely timing cover on these models, which was no longer able to carry the triangular patent plate, came in two sections, as a panel was cut from the rear of the cover which, when unbolted, gave access to the bolts securing the starter motor. Electric-start T140s were given gold 'Electro' transfers on the lower front of their side panels, with a bolt of lightning through the last letter.

On the T140ES, sensibly the rest of the electrical gear was also uprated. A larger 14.5 amp hour Yuasa battery required a revised mounting and a bump in the seat pan, and was used in conjunction with a higher output RM24 180-watt alternator with a 14 amp Stator, and a triple Zener diode pack. The electronic ignition's reluctor and amplifier were also suitably amended. T140ES models retained their kickstarts at first, and although the penalties for push-button starting included a weight gain of over 30lb (13.6kg) (they were catalogued at 430lb/195kg dry), and a price rise of £100 to £1,868, the starter worked, and the model proved popular, making up more than half of Meriden's remaining production.

The early versions went out as stock Bonnevilles, but from June 1980, the starter was also offered on a new touring variant, the T140EX Executive, which had been available in kick-start form since February 1980. It was aimed at BMW's market segment, and emphasised this fact by coming in either red or

An early 1980 T140EX Executive. There is no electric foot, but there is an early screen, neat luggage, and spiffy Smoked Burgundy finish.

blue imitations of the 'smoked' paint finishes then found on the *Meisterschaft* twins. The Executive had a capacious glassfibre handlebar fairing, with screens at first clear but later tinted and trimmed with black around their upper edge, and lined inside with ABS leather grain material. There were matching Sigma panniers and a top box, all colour co-ordinated, and twin round mirrors, which were soon to be found on the rest of the range. The handlebars were large police model pull-backs, and the seat was initially a sculpted 'king and queen' variant of the D's, although a standard '79 seat could also be ordered. The T140EX was equipped with the first examples of the new European made, 4-gallon tank. Colour schemes involved Smoked Blue or Smoked Burgundy (by far the more attractive and numerous option) darkening from bright to

near black on the tank, mudguards and side panels. For UK versions this was highlighted by a single L-shaped gold line on the lower edges of the tank, side panels and panniers.

The contracted US market meant the factory was awash with US components, and so for 1980–81 Meriden offered in the UK, a version of the T140E with or without electric foot, dubbed the Bonneville American. This differed from the actual US export models in fitting fork gaiters, the plain name badge on its tank rather than the 'picture-frame' badge, and the previous year's seats, where the US export models fitted the D-style seat. Finish on the American's US tank involved both top and bottom 'scallops'. They and the genuine US export models were offered carrying either black tanks with gold-lined Candy Apple Red 'scallops', or Olympic Flame with gold-lined black 'scallops'. The UK

The T140E(S) Bonneville 'American' Electro in its most popular colours. The 1981 Bonnie was voted *Motor Cycle News*'s 'Machine of the Year'.

Machine of the Year
Bonneville 750

models came in either Steel Grey with a Candy Apple red 'zig-zag', with a black inner and outer stripe sandwiching red, or all-black with double white stripes. Side panels for all these models were now black.

In **1981** the co-op attempted to capitalise on its reduced circumstances and component services by adopting the notion of bespoke bikes, ie the twins could be ordered in any combination of what was available, with machines so concocted bearing an 'FFC' engine number prefix, for Factory Fitted Custom. The Meriden men kept punching though, offering a limited edition angled at one of that year's big stories, the wedding of Prince Charles and Lady Diana.

Some more useful improvements came, as well as a significantly increased proportion of

European-sourced components on the remaining Bonnevilles. In the engine, the timing side main bearing became a stronger, four-lipped roller. The traditionally rapid-wear inlet valves were fitted with oil seals, which also had a good effect in reducing oil consumption. Pressure oil feed to the tappets was discarded, so both inlet and exhaust cam followers became interchangeable. The starter motor had blocked the use of the TDC plug, so this moved to the front of the crankcase, and the mating notch on the fly wheel was altered to suit. The clutch action was lightened both by modification of the operating mechanism, and by the use of lighter, T120 springs plus the reduction of the number of drive plates from seven to six. In conjunction with new nylon-lined cables, this significantly improved clutch

The UK T140E(S) for 1981 – by then a fairly well-sorted, if expensive, machine.

operation. The Bonneville's Concentric Mk 2 carburettors were given larger needle jets, as well as a handlebar-mounted choke lever. Early in the model year, the UK model T140's gearing was sensibly raised by the substitution of a 45-tooth rear sprocket for the previous 47T. Finally, in a welcome move, screw-in exhaust stubs were fitted to the cylinder head again, with the pipes a 'push-over' fit on them, and finned exhaust clamps completing the picture.

New, rubber-mounted footrests were fitted, as well as an anti-vibration fork shroud allowing the use of a 60/45-watt sealed-beam headlamp unit. A pair of round mirrors sourced in Germany appeared on all Bonnies. Most 1981 T140s came with a version of the D's dual seat, although some appeared with the previous one. Early on, chromed mudguards were replaced by polished stainless steel ones. On electric start models, the kick-start became an optional extra. In mid-year, the brakes were revised with the discs becoming unplated cast iron, so that sintered Dunlopads could be used, and wet weather performance improved. On some models the calipers became Dural

forgings, black-painted and lacking the previous chromed covers. Twin cast iron AP Racing front discs were offered as an option which became high on every Triumph owner's wish-list, not just for the extra stopping power, but because their balance reduced fork twist.

From around April 1981, in response to tightening emission regulations in the US and elsewhere, the Concentric Mk 2 carburettors began to be replaced by German Bing Type 94 constant velocity instruments, produced in collaboration with Amal. The Bings required extended side panels to protect their linkages, and these panels were decorated with a single gold line swooping up under the name badge. The optional cast wheels changed from Lester to Morris ones, also seven-spoked. The winkers changed progressively from the chromed Lucas type to black, squared-off German ones on black stalks which kept them where they were meant to be. Most significantly, during the year, with traditional tank-maker Homers of Birmingham going out of business, both UK and US petrol tanks changed to Italian-made versions. These had deeper, rounded sides and a smoother, more modern profile, but Triumphs lost something, although the tank's hinged, lockable Monza-type flip-up caps were welcome. These tanks

The black and silver 1981 UK T140LE Royal Wedding featured in a Maker's Eye design exhibition.

all came with the simple Triumph badge.

No less than six finish options were offered, all in either UK or US spec, although probably only the Smoked Blue and Smoked Flame versions actually went to America. Except on the smoked finishes, all side panels were black, so it was only the petrol tank that varied in colour. On the UK models, the previous year's all-black plus grey and red were joined by black and double gold-striped Candy Apple red, and by Silver Blue with black 'zig-zags', with black outer and gold inner lining. There were no 'zig-zags' on the Smoked Blue or Smoked Flame finishes, where the paint was disposed as on the Executive, including the single, low gold line on the tank, as well as on the panels when these covered the Bing carbs. The US models carried the same colour range, with both upper and lower 'scallops' this year, in the stubbier form seen on the US T140D. Where the 'picture-frame' badges were used, they were in plain polished chrome, rather than

with a white-painted background.

The special model, in two very different styles and a short run coda, was the T140LE (for limited edition) Royal Wedding, which coincided with the event itself in July 1981. Just 250 were built in all. Both versions featured the first chrome tanks to come out of Meriden in 25 years, and all Royal Wedding models were electric start. The UK version had a silver-painted frame, including the centre and prop stands, to contrast with an engine finished completely in matt black, with just polished fin edges on the cylinder head, rocker box and points cover. The ungaitered forks featured, as the whole '82 range would do, black sliders and top covers, as well as black ears for a black headlamp shell, and black instrument cups. Double front discs, Morris wheels and Bing carburettors were standard, as was a kick-starter. The stunning chromed 4-gallon tank featured skinny upper and lower black 'scallops' lined in gold, plus the big black side

The UK T140LE with a chromed tank, silver frame, black engine and polished fin edges really was a limited edition.

panels with the sloping gold line and the words 'Limited Edition' at their lower rear end. Unique touches were three-fold: a tank-top bung bearing 'Royal Wedding 1981' and a stylised version of the Prince of Wales emblematic feathers; a Palace-approved special head-stem plate showing the machine's limited edition number; and side panel badges, black on the UK, blue on the US, with beneath 'Bonneville' the word Royal and a chrome crown insignia. A special certificate came with each bike.

The US version, which Gaylin avers never went to the States, was rather different. Where the UK wore a black D-type seat, the US sported a 'king and queen' as on the Executive, only garishly finished with black sides but with the seat portions in light grey. The US frame was black and virtually everything else shone – the cylinders were silver-painted, the crankcase outer covers were highly polished, as were the fork's top covers and lower members. Chrome on the headlamp shell and mounting brackets,

instrument binnacles, brake pedal, side stand, rear sprocket plate, the stems of the German winkers and even the plug caps, left just the centre stand black as well as the springs on the rear units. These, like the UK's (which had chromed springs) were the new and superior Marzocchi remote reservoir units, with a sealed air chamber and five-way spring pre-load. Concentric Mk 2s were fitted, and the chromed US tanks were the old-style 'slimline' ones, with a round cap and the chromed 'picture-frame' badge. They were finished with slim upper and truncated lower gold-lined 'scallops', plus a gold-lined top panel, all coloured like the side panels, in Smoked Candy Permanent Blue. Wire wheels and a single disc were the final distinguishing US features. Love 'em or loath 'em, these were stunning looking motorcycles.

The coda came with the further 50-odd machines actually exported to the States, apparently just called 'Royal' without the 'Wedding'. They came with a black-painted UK

The US T140LE Royal (Wedding) was rather different.

The 1981 US Royal was a seriously shiney machine with a funny seat.

Some of the last of the UK-built 'slimline' tanks went on the US Royals.

European tank with its edges surrounded by a double gold stripe and black side panels for the Bing carbs with a single diagonal gold line. The top half of the engine was black but the crankcase was unpainted and the outer covers polished. Either spoked or Morris wheels were provided, with double front discs, low bars and the D-type seat.

The last full production year, **1982**, as mentioned, brought the Marzocchi rear units and forks with black sliders and top covers, as well as a right-side fork slider modified to take a second caliper if double discs were fitted. All models were by now fitted with high-output alternators. T140ES Electros sold to America had new, more moderate 6½in (165mm) rise handlebars, but US models in the UK used up the 8½in (215mm) chopper-style ones. During the year, Magura dog-leg control levers were

The 1982 T140ES Electro, with European-made tank, instruments, winkers, mirrors and rear shocks.

The final, 1982 electric-start version of the T140EX Executive.

The '82 black TSS eight-valve 750 – a promising design insufficiently developed.

fitted and brought a big reduction to the finger-stretch needed on the controls. The long 'Bing' side panels were fastened on by a single Allen screw each, and no connecting spring. The 4-gallon Italian tank was now used for all, simply painted differently for varying models.

The reduced and debt-ridden co-op nevertheless had plans for the future, including a move from the half-empty Meriden works with its high overheads, and a projected model range led by a 900cc DOHC twin, with the traditional twins alongside it for a while, mounted in an anti-vibration (AV) frame. A few of the AV-framed Bonnevilles were produced, but since they were police and prototype machines only, are beyond the scope of this book.

However, another strand in the co-op's forward plans did get into production in 1982. This was the eight-valve TSS, launched in March 1982. It had been developed from the 1960s' Weslake conversion for 650 Triumphs. One problem with the latter had been the way it had stressed the stock twins' bottom end, so although the TSS had a stock electric start crankcase and gearbox, within the cases lay a shorter, stiffer one-piece crankshaft with larger diameter, narrower big-end journals, permitting stronger lateral webbing. The crank, including its cheeks, was carefully machined, and this both helped reduce vibration and permitted Triumph's 'never go more than 7' (,000rpm) rule of thumb to be stretched safely to 10,000rpm.

The extra power was available because each of the conventional pair of pushrods in the head operated a pair of rockers, working the eight valves, since the rockers were now forked. In place of the previous hemispherical combustion chambers with their dome-topped pistons, the TSS chambers were shallower and the pistons flat-topped with valve cutaways, giving 9.5:1 cr but still running cooler than the standard ones. The valves themselves could now be set at a much narrower (30°) angle than the conventionally widely set arrangement with its somewhat restricted breathing. Parallel inlet tracts were fed by 34mm Amal Mk 2s for the UK, and Bings for the US. Another aid to cool running, was, finally, a closely finned, squared-

The plainly styled all-alloy eight-valve TSS engine produced 57bhp.

off cylinder block in alloy. In this, the distance between the bores of the cylinders with their steel liners had been widened to give better air space. The con rods were redesigned to suit, and 10 holding-down studs, four of them running straight through into the crankcase, kept things together. Cooper sealing rings, rather than a gasket, were employed for head sealing, due to the restricted space from the wide-set bores. The net result of the all-alloy eight-valve engine was an 8lb (3.6kg) weight saving, a claimed output of 57bhp at 6,500rpm, and top speeds on test regularly in excess of 120mph (193kph).

The TSS engine was all-black barring polished covers and polished fin edges. Otherwise, running gear was as for the other

1982 T140s, with double discs as standard. Finish was all-black with double gold lining on the tank, or black with Candy Apple Red gold-lined upper and lower 'scallops', plus TSS side panel badges on panels finished in matt black lower and gloss upper, the two divided by a single gold line. Gearing had been raised by the use of a 43-tooth rear sprocket, and while this put the standing quarter times above the 14 second mark, it gave running with greatly reduced vibration up to 85mph (137kph). While most of the power was at the top end, the engine proved unfussy, and noticeably quicker than that of a T140. Sadly, the model had been rushed into production prematurely. The first batch of cylinder heads were porous, the Cooper ring design was flawed and blew frequently, and the steel liners slipped down the alloy barrels – these were only some of the problems before time ran out. A pity, because I have ridden a modified, carefully built TSS that was as fast, smooth and exciting as a good Bonneville should be, only more so.

That left just one model to go, the TSX Custom launched in 1982, a T140ES decked with mildly exotic cycle parts and a screaming mimi paint job which aped contemporary Yamaha Factory Customs, to create a loud-

Firing up a TSS might-have-been, which went as well as any twin the author has ever ridden.

The 1982 TSX Factory Custom, a chunky cruiser.

Just as well the TSX was loud, because after 1982, for Meriden, the rest was silence.

looking, chunky cruiser. In the engine the crankshaft bob weights were machined on the sides as the TSS's had been, and the motor was painted black above the crankcases. Gearing was lowered by reverting to a 47-tooth rear sprocket. The engine breathed through 32mm Bing carbs, and these were exposed by new cut-back side panels carrying a cast metal TSX badge.

The wheels were Morris mag alloys, shod with an Avon Speedmaster front and Roadrunner rear with their names picked out in white, 3.25 x 19in front and a whopping 5.10 x 16in rear. This fat rear cover meant the swinging arm had to be widened, the speedo drive revised and a chunk removed from the rear chainguard, which was chromed. The rear mudguard looked smaller than it was due to a cunning use of plastic, and the low-rider illusion was helped along by a fat low-look dual seat and by chrome-spring Paioli shock absorbers angled forward. This was done by putting their rear mounting points back 2in, directly above the wheel spindle. As with the T140D, the substantial seat rather undercut the bike's lean 'n' mean styling pretensions. The front end was kicked up on ungaitered forks with chrome top covers and polished alloy sliders, holding between them, a short painted front mudguard, and a chrome headlamp shell on chromed bent wire mountings. The exhaust system featured fat, 1¾in pipes, unlinked at the head, angling out and down to shorty megaphone silencers with restrictive internals to satisfy US noise regs, and finally linked by an inconspicuous tube passing under the frame.

Brakes were single discs, the rear one operated by double Brembo callipers with chrome covers as at the front.

The petrol tank was the recently introduced Italian-built 3.6 (US) gallon version of the US tank, with a circular filler cap, plain Triumph badges, and a single fuel tap with cross-over balance pipe. This tank, finished in metallic Burgundy, was then decorated with a vivid decal comprised of curved red, orange and yellow bands, inconspicuously bordered with a double gold line at the front, single at the rear. The same three colours were echoed in curved transfers below the angled metal badge on the side panels. On test with *CBG*, the changes to the geometry were found to have removed some of the Bonnie's stability in fast (65+mph/105+kph) corners, but this was not felt to be crucial. The TSX proved a pleasant bike to cruise between 60 and 85mph (96–137kph), with speed tapering off in the mid-nineties (c150kph), mainly thanks to the restrictive silencers.

The last machines were produced at Meriden during January **1983**. The previous months had often seen them in mix 'n' match mode, for as John Nelson wrote, 'at the bitter end it was "anything goes" for instant cash.' Finishes for 1982 had included for the UK American variants two new schemes, Smoked Blue with upper only gold-lined Silver 'scallops', and

The Harris-built T140 Bonneville UK, with many foreign components including nice upswept Lafranconi silencers.

Smoked Flame with gold-lined off-white upper 'scallops', both with colour co-ordinated side panels. But by far the most popular finish was Black with gold-lined Candy Apple Red slim-winged 'scallops' as on the UK 'Royal Wedding', as well as Pale Blue with similar gold-lined Black 'scallops', both with black side panels. US export bikes went out in Smoked Blue or Smoked Flame, with no tank 'scallops' but a single gold pinstripe around the forward contours of the tank on each side. For the rump of 1983, most bikes were in black with the double slim-winged gold-lined 'scallops' in Candy Apple Red.

After the co-op had gone into liquidation, building magnate John Bloor picked up the Triumph name and manufacturing rights. Les Harris, a prominent manufacturer and supplier of Triumph pattern spares, was granted a licence to manufacture T140 Bonnevilles to Meriden specification, at his factory near Newton Abbot in Devon. The first of some

1,200 of these appeared nearly two years later, in June **1985**, the delay being partly due to Bloor's insistence that these Bonnevilles should conform strictly to the Meriden product, when Harris had been hoping to use the stronger TSS crank and German-made Nikasil alloy barrels. But in fact, as he later put it, 'members of the staff might have inadvertently let some out with the alloy barrels or TSS cranks held in stock' – so some owners of Harris-built machines got lucky!

Otherwise, while the basic machine was unchanged apart from a TSX-style crank with machined bobweight sides, many more components were now sourced abroad. These included Radaelli wheel rims, Paioli 38mm stanchion forks and rear units, and brakes (including twin discs at the front) by Brembo, as well as the quieter silencers, which gave more ground clearance, from Lafranconi. The carbs, however, were Amal 1⅛s, ie Mk 1 Concentric bodies with Mk 2 cold start slides. The side

The last gasp. A Devon-built Bonneville in US guise, although none was exported.

panels were the cutaway TSX type, held together by a single rubber band. There were mixed reports about the finish, specifically on the Italian suspension components, but the Devon bikes were reported as smoother than their predecessors and could still make 115mph (185kph). The last was produced in March 1988.

The oil-in-frame Bonnie's initial troubles, difficult production history and failure to remain competitive with current levels of motorcycle performance and reliability, can easily blind one to the fact that both 650s and 750s could still be very satisfying bikes. As always with the Bonneville, owners and aftermarket suppliers found ways of improving and uprating them, particularly the T140. In 1978 Steve Trasler, on Triumph dealer Bennett & Son's T140, won the Avon/Bike championship for road-legal machines, in the process beating off some very determined Kawasaki, Honda and Laverda-mounted opposition. (The Trasler racing bike engines use the earlier splayed heads, and

Brian Bennett recently revealed that the oil-bearing frame had been modified to take 8 pints, and that the biggest problem had been the swinging arm pivot, which they had finally and successfully reinforced with an extra gusset.) So there was life in the old dog yet, and as late as 1981, readers voted the T140 *MCN*'s Machine of the Year. Limited, high quality production of a developed Triumph twin could probably have survived, Morgan-like, to this day. The 750, however, will never carry the cachet of the pre-units or the 1960's T120s, because it was never as competitive or charismatic in its day, as downright hot, as they had been; the de-tuned origins of the 750 motor made sure that it could rarely be the roadburner of old. In fact, one of both the kindest and cruellest things written about the T140 came in a retrospective test of a '78 model in *Classic Bike*, where they concluded: 'The T140V felt far too good-natured to be a Bonneville.'

How many roads?

During its 30-year production life and after, the Bonnie was both a magnetic icon and a ubiquitous part of the everyday scene. Triumph's greatest hit intertwined itself with many lives in many ways, from short-haul blasts to long-distance travels, from manufacture to sales, service and specials building.

So here are some voices from that long love affair between a multitude of young men and women, and 'the best motorcycle in the World.'

Bob Innes was a rocker and a fast man in the 1950s. '60s and '70s. With a partner he ran a London bike shop called Northwest Autos, and as well as sponsoring racers, was well respected as a builder of specials, often Bonneville-powered, like *Ghengis Khan*, or a supercharged '66 T120 in a '55 Norton frame. Today, he keeps his hand in doing engine jobs at long-established dealers Rex Judd, (where the final Bonneville builder, Les Harris, once worked as a storeman).

'I was at Rex Judd's today, and the lads there were going on about how the Suzuki TLS, a 1,000cc vee-twin, didn't handle, because its front wheel lifted under power. Blimey, I told 'em, you don't know what bikes used to be, in respect of handling. When the Bonnie came out in '59, that was a diabolical thing. Looking back it's amazing anyone survived – they were

bendy old things. But we all loved 'em, they were quick. That's why we all bought them. It was such a varied bike in all its guises. The '59 Tangerine and Pearl I think was one of the best colours.

'At the Ace Café, until around '54 or '55 the majority of fast bikes had been retired racers, 7Rs, Mk VIII cammy Velos, single cam Nortons. Then the Triumph started becoming the thing. They just had the appeal. They were reasonably cheap, you could get the spares, and they could be tuned – and they certainly had the mystique. Triumphs were the most popular.

'We thought it was fun to strip off the lights like a racer. I'd steal so many of my mum's frying pans, cut the handles off, and they'd look like Manx number plates – to us, at any rate. We'd put a cycle headlamp on the bike and go down the Watford bypass at night – three lanes with the suicide lane in the middle, the only way to keep going was to find the cat's eyes, drrt, drrt, drrt, – you knew by the sound you were OK!

'I never bought a Bonnie new, with the workshop I'd get damaged bikes or ones needing work. Because I had the shop I went through all the range virtually. I had a '66, which I remember was quite a nice one. If you had a Bonnie you had to have fairly strong wrists. If you had a good one, we used to

upgrade the clutch springs; there were square ones, they might have been speedway ones from Jacksons just down the road. And here's a thing that's never mentioned about the early Bonnies, but I knew because at the shop I took enough back; they plated the spokes, and the rear wheels used to collapse. They went to normal spokes after that. It hadn't exactly enhanced the handling!

'The best Bonnie-engine racing special I ever did was the way the factory should have gone, I always reckoned. At the end of development I got it down to about 250lb [113kg]. One time at Crystal Palace, Percy Tait came over to us after a race and said, "Bloody hell, that's bloody quick, *and* it handles."

'ARE alloy barrels were a fair old weight saver. I'd play with valve timing, even made up my own cams, and had 'em case-hardened. On one bike I tried the same valve timing as a 350 Gold Star, and it did go quite well. I got my Triumphs to rev to 8,000. I used to lighten the flywheels – I know they did it on the '66 bikes, but I think the factory would have freaked out if they'd seen mine! Here's a photo of one blown up, with the flywheels hanging out – that's what happens if you don't change the rods regularly. I used to do engines for loads of different people, mainly club racers. I did have some success. I never had any trouble with heads warping and so on. I think a lot of the trouble in those days was people never warmed them up. And people who brought their bikes in when I had the shop never used to have changed the oil.

'The big let-down with the Triumph engine was the pushrod tubes – why did they never cast them into the barrels? (The other big let-down was the 750…) But when they went to the oil-in-frame, the Bonnie lost something. For me, if they'd used alloy barrels, enclosed the pushrod tubes, made the head like a CB175 with a big inspection plate, Triumph could have soldiered on that way.

'To me the fun of motorcycling is taking a bike like the Bonnie and riding it to its limit, the silencers all smashed in and the footrests all bent up; the satisfaction. But you can't do that with today's machines.'

Bill Crosby runs the well-known British bike and Triumph specialist shop Reg Allen in West London, and has recently opened the London Motorcycle Museum at Greenford. The museum, which is well worth a visit, is something of a shrine to Triumphs, with many fascinating prototypes and racers on display, as well as the last Meriden-built Bonneville. Another ace habitué who lost a leg in a bike crash in the 1950s, Bill, a shrewd, down-to-earth character, here recalls his days selling new Bonnevilles.

'We've been at Reg Allen since '58, but we didn't sell so many Triumphs in the Sixties because we didn't have an agency – if we wanted a Bonnie we got one from Whitbys of Acton. The Bonnie ruled the roost then – if you wanted to go up the Ace or Brands Hatch, there might be Velocette or Ariel enthusiasts there, but Triumphs had the edge. The company's problem was they were so successful with the Bonneville that they didn't bring out the triple in '65, when the prototype P1 which we have at the museum was up and running, and that could have saved them.

'The Sixties T120s we used to race! We were scrambling them 52 weekends a year and sometimes at three events over a single holiday weekend. Triumphs were reasonably cheap to maintain, and if you blew one up, the engines were relatively cheap to buy. With the Bonnie's twin carbs, all you could gain was about 6–8mph [10–13kph] at the top end; with two riders together on single and twin carb bikes, you'd be pushed to tell the difference between them. The name was magic. Because they sold

so well in the States, everyone had to have one, even though they knew that tweaking twin carbs was a pain; most of them were running around on 1½ cylinders, when a single carb would have sorted it. But they gotta have a Bonnie!

'They did require a bit of maintenance, especially the electrics, but once the warranty was out, I think it was six months, most riders did their own. Most bikes then were on HP. The Grand Union Canal is just behind here, and lads who couldn't keep up their payments used to ride them into it and get the insurance. Not so much Bonnies though. They were *the* bikes to steal.

'In the Sixties, customers were mainly satisfied with them. They didn't seem to have the same warranty problems as they did with the first co-op bikes, which were pretty disastrously leaky, the so-called *Torrey Canyons*. The co-op finally got them right, then the TSS knocked them for six – which was not their fault (the porous heads); they'd had bikes out on the road for a couple of years to prove it, let alone Weslake having been on the tracks for years.

'In the Seventies, NVT while they were marketing them, didn't seem to want to talk to anybody. We were servicing the AA's 750s, and they wanted higher output batteries for the bikes, so they could recharge car batteries. We went up to the Earl's Court Show and wanted to ask about it. The co-op workers were manning the Triumph stand, but no-one from NVT would come out. They were all behind a screen, drinking.

'We had big problems getting the agency for Triumphs in '76/'77. We'd arranged the finance, gone up to Meriden two or three times, but nothing. The Abbey Garage at Hillingdon were the blue-eyed boys. I'd built a boat at Shepperton, *Pandora*, and I used to look out for the boat next to it, which belonged to a managing director. When I told him about this situation, his advice was, "Go to the top". The co-op had just got a £1 million loan from GEC, so I went to their Chairman, Lord Weinstock. I phoned up and got his PA, who said the co-op can't do that, turn down money – I'll see that they'll be in touch by 4.30 that afternoon. They

weren't, but the next morning Bob Haines from Meriden was on the phone, and after the weekend we got our first bikes.

'The 750 Bonneville was a different bike, because it didn't rev like the 650. But once the *Torrey Canyon* image was cleared up, they handled well, the brakes were quite good, and everyone was pretty happy with them. In 1978, we had 15 T140s lined up outside the shop. They were all painted in lovely colours, though the co-op never seemed to give the colours proper names and numbers. The blues particularly used to be different every batch, and the flashes on them varied – and the thickness of the gold lining!

'We used to maintain David Essex's T140 which had a chromed tank – the co-op had given him a Bonneville, and one to James Hunt, who had just hacked around on it a bit and then sold it on. The customer who bought it was steered our way by Harry Woolridge, who was then the co-op's warranty officer. The bike had a misfire just off tickover, like all the Mk 2 Concentric bikes – they all did it; and that was just the start …

'But the main problem before the factory closed was duff pattern spares. You could never make the co-op understand about spares; if you wanted 25 US clutch cables, they had to take them off production bikes. They didn't have the money. By the end they were paying out so much for rates etc, you could go up there and they would sell you anything…'

Bill Crosby mentioned **Bob Haines**, a Coventry man and an industry stalwart who started at Meriden in 1961 as a production road tester.

'When I started, new testers had to ride the small bikes, Tiger Cubs etc, and you turned out of the factory gates to the right, towards Allesley. After six months you got the big bikes and you'd turn left out of the gates, through Meriden village and down the Straight Mile. You'd do your test run and then park up in a layby and set the carbs, ride back to the factory, pass the motorcycle off and take another. There were about 15 of us, every bike had to be road tested, and we'd each try to do 10 to 12 machines a day.

'In the Sixties, the Bonnies were pretty good,

Bill Crosby today, at the London Motorcycle Museum.

with few problems – the engines were bulletproof. The Triumph twin engine went ever so well, but in the very early Sixties when I started, they didn't handle – they used to shake their heads as we always said. Then, after I'd been there a year, Doug Hele and Brian Jones came from Norton, and adjusted the head angles. The early unit T120s were great bikes, their problem was their brakes. Then, in '68 we got Hele's leading-shoe brake and better forks. The late Sixties' T120s were really good bikes, with just the occasional electrical problem. When they went to the smaller Siba coil, its centre sat in pitch instead of oil, and we had a lot of trouble with them suffering from vibration. On test they usually went on to one cylinder – fortunately not both. Eventually the coils had to be rubber mounted.

'Then suddenly, the oil-in-frame arrived. Up until then, as I said, the bikes had been bulletproof, and given little trouble on the assembly track. Umberslade Hall got the idea of the o-i-f from the works BSA Victor scramblers, which had oil-bearing chassis. I'm 6ft 2in, so the 34in seat height didn't bother me. There was a tester called Bill 'the Binder' Hemmings, a short guy, who couldn't get on the P39 – it was a standing joke. In early 1972, I was working in Experimental, and I and a Cornish apprentice called Fred were asked by Bert Hopwood and Doug Hele to stop over one weekend, and with instructions from the drawing office, we lowered the frame's seat height. By Monday we'd done it.

'Another problem with the P39's beam frame was that you couldn't draw the head-to-barrel bolt out of the barrel, because there wasn't room. It had to be a short bolt, which came out

Bob Haines worked in the Meriden Comp Shop, fettling off-road twins like this one, shown with works rider Gordon Farley.

of another insert in the barrel – a two-tier bolt. So you could draw the short one out, then put a special tool down and draw the second one out to remove the barrel. That arrangement stayed on the Bonneville until the end.

'With the T140, the problem was that the quick conversion to 750 had left a thin gap between the two pots, and normal gaskets couldn't cope – they were forever blowing head gaskets. In the end, in 1978, we went to Perkins Diesels, and got a composite gasket which

cost £2.50 trade when the other one had been 50p. But it did put it right.

'I think a lot of the T140's vibration problems came from the balancing. In the old days the operatives had been skilled, they knew how to work the machinery and do it properly, but when they were replaced, that was when there was a real problem with big twin vibration. When GEC were helping us, they had a factory at Stoke making huge generators, some of them 50ft (15.25m) long, and they sent a

Top tester Percy Tait was not the tallest of men – so did he appreciate the P39's 34½in seat height?

vibration expert from there to Meriden. He said we needed a balancer shaft; Doug Hele had already designed one, but he had gone by then, and the expert said "bring an engine to Stoke, ask for me, we'll sort it out." They built a one-off, and you know the test, well you could stand 50p on its end on the tank with that engine running, and it never moved. But with the shaft in the engine you lost 10mph, and the 750 was already down on performance against the 650, so it was never made.'

John South is a fast rider with a particular passion for Meriden triples, which his career in computers today has allowed him to indulge. He owns, among others, a Slippery Sam replica, a Rocket 3, and no less than three X75 Hurricanes. But when he and his partner decided it was time to hit the long roads, it was a T140 Bonneville which took them from Norway to Greece. John thinks 'Every home should have one'.

A lot of riders dream about how nice it would

be to take the old bike South for a summer away from it all, but in 1985 John South and his then girlfriend Jane actually did it. They covered 12,000 miles and took in 18 countries, just a man, a woman, a motorcycle and a very small tent, surviving mechanical mayhem and savage weather – as well as some industrial strength hangovers.

Jane was a nurse and John, as mentioned, works in computers. He's a wirey, jokey individual originating from the Cheshire/Derbyshire border, with his fair share of Northern grit. Jane did some of the driving, as the Triumph was her bike. It features a cut-down seat, as she is not the tallest person in the world. The choice of the Triumph twin for the big trip was deliberate. The 750 twins may not be famous for reliability, but they are light, simple to work on and sturdy enough.

Originally a 1978 US spec 750 Bonneville, preliminary work included fitting twin front discs to cope with the touring weight, a 4-gallon tank and a Tiger single-carb head – acquired for £75 new, and run with one of the Bonnie's carburettors suitably jetted up. The head turned out to need new exhaust pipes, and the matching airbox turned out to be for a 650 and didn't line up, but once installed the set-up ran perfectly, and payed for itself in petrol saved.

The Triumph had done 14,000 miles at the start. It was given a complete and thorough overhaul, and as usual, almost the only problems were to be with areas that had been touched or with parts which had been replaced. These included clutch and throttle cables which went within 2,000 miles. They were replaced by the originals, which have lasted to this day. Luggage mainly went into a two-tier tank bag and in Krauser panniers, with their rack system grafted over a Craven rack for greater strength. If the luggage was good, they were amiably disorganised in another area, namely cold and wet weather gear. As Jane put it, 'Which was more stupid; not taking enough clothes, or the silly little tent?' In the interest of seeing everything and anticipating hot weather, John also elected to ride in an open-face helmet, with no visor.

After a shakedown run through Scotland, the Isle of Man for the TT, and Ireland, the couple took a ship in July for Norway. The omens were not outstanding as, on the ferry, John's capped front tooth fell out, so he spent the next few days looking like Worzel Gummidge.

Norway offered magnificent scenery, and several days' rain. This was dispiriting, because to be able to spend months on the road, they had to keep the budget tight: £150 a week was the maximum for everything, including petrol, ferries, etc. This meant baked bean cuisine and left little slack for amusement, or for taking refuge in hotels.

When the rain cleared they took to the hills. Road surfaces varied a lot, and the weight of the loaded bike made itself felt with wheelies coming out of uphill corners, even after the toolbag had been slung under the headlamp (where it dinged the front mudguard). The fjords and mountains were vast and breathtaking; on one occasion they switched off and free-wheeled, hitting 70mph with no power, for seven miles – 'that's the magnitude you're talking'.

Then they headed for Sweden ('up Norway and turn right'). Once there, they rounded a bend in the middle of a pine forest to meet a Volvo coming head on at them on the crown of the road. Instinct took over; John pulled left, like he would have in England, as the Volvo swung the same way, getting back on its correct side of the road. They missed by about 18in [500mm], with the Volvo losing control and skidding off the road and on to gravel as the Triumph headed into the trees. John was angry enough to chase and catch the driver, and 'had something to say' to the woman at the wheel, until she managed to explain that out in the country in Sweden, driving in the middle of the road was accepted practice to avoid the moose, as collision with the animals caused more accidents than other cars.

They headed south at a deliberately leisurely pace, rarely covering more than 100 miles [160km] a day. That left plenty of time each day to get camp set up and go walking and sightseeing, which was the way they wanted it. They also avoided cities most of the time. Then, skirting Hamburg, serious mechanical gremlins struck. The centre nut of the clutch unscrewed itself, allowing the clutch to slip badly as its

John South on his Bonnie in 1985 watching a Porsche rally in Pula, Yugoslavia. This was communism?

centre was trying to spin on the mainshaft. Typically, the correct size socket for it was one item they weren't carrying, so it was tightened up with the available tools, and the pair proceeded over the Dutch border to some rather memorable R&R in Amsterdam.

Belgium came next which provided another first – motorways with potholes. Then it was over the border to Germany again, to stay with some biker friends met in Ireland and get an all-round overhaul for man and machine. The spokes of the rear wheel were showing distress, so they were replaced with Husquvarna ones. The rear tyre, a large block-tread, square section Dunlop, had suffered badly in Norway, so was replaced with a Roadrunner to match the front one, which lasted the whole distance. On stripping, the clutch mainshaft proved to be scored yet serviceable, but its Woodruff key had been destroyed. The key was replaced with one off a

BMW, but the clutch inner had gone, badly, and needed replacing.

Parts were ordered from Frankfurt at 3pm and arrived as promised at 8.30 the following morning. Yes, in Germany 'Ze Triumph parts ran on time'. An engineering shop with a press was found, to dismantle and reassemble the centre. Most importantly of all, John got his tooth, which he'd hung onto all the way, replaced with the aid of a special compound superglue.

Switzerland followed, staying with family friends and walking in the mountains, and then Austria, but by then autumn was coming, and they were seized with the urge to run to the sun. At the foot of the Grossglockner pass over to Yugoslavia, they put on all the clothes they could, cagouls over leather jackets, and set off up the mountain, but soon they were stopping every few miles because of the pain of the cold, especially on John's exposed face. Then, halfway up, the back wheel suffered a puncture. Using an adaptor on the bicycle pump they carried, they pumped it up and rode back down again. They were carrying only one spare inner tube – a 19in one which would serve both wheels at a pinch. But in town they found a can of Finilec. It worked, and the bike ran that way for the whole trip.

So they climbed the pass, which was brilliant, although the Triumph did run out of puff a little towards the top, which was negotiated in second and even first gears. Then the magnificent view unfolded from the summit, with the ocean a faint blue line a hundred miles below in the distance, and they rode down into the warm. They camped outside Pula, enjoyed the cheap wine and basked in the blissful heat, although it carried 'tropical hazards' – the food was sub-standard, they got the runs and the ground was too hard to bang tent pegs into. Talking to a rider who had just come up they decided that five days on the Yugoslav roads down to Greece was probably not a good idea, so they splashed out on a ferry from Rijeka to Corfu. It cost £98, but that was with a cabin and all meals, and they enjoyed the contrast between roughing it in rural Yugoslavia, and dinner with full service in the rather luxurious ex-DFDS ferry.

On Corfu they fell in with an American on a BMW, and being late in the season, John negotiated with a lady who looked after villas and got them into an unused one in the north of the island for £1.50 a night. It was only a few hundred yards from an empty beach, where a taverna owner kept his establishment open solely for their benefit, and they spent an idyllic six weeks in 'super-relax mode', drinking Retzina by the crate and eating the fish the bar owner went out and caught every morning.

The Triumph meanwhile was biding its time, and on the way to the ferry, after 2,000 miles, the repaired clutch gave up the ghost. The American towed them to the boat, and in Patras on mainland Greece, they met Andreas, a local DJ and owner of probably the tastiest Triumph in Greece. John and Jane visited Istanbul while parts were being sent from England, and then despite the arrival of an incorrectly bored mainshaft, with Andreas's help, effective repairs

were carried out. The Greek's primary chaincase had been welded, so John exchanged it for his own pristine case, as the least he could do.

Time had passed, and it was early November when they arrived in Brindisi to find the weather had changed from the 20° in Patras to a near-freezing 6°. An epic struggle home began, with the lack of clothing leading to John wrapping his hands in their first aid bandages and putting bin liners over his boots and the handlebars. On the Mediterranean autostradas, terrifying winds nearly blew them off the high road bridges. Very wisely by now John had broken out the emergency Barclaycard so the motto was 'Hell by day, luxury by night', as they went to ground in four-star motels each evening. Then, in France, with 600 miles to go, it started to snow. The motorway went from three lanes to two, to one. On the worst day, they only managed 85 miles, and the next morning the frozen throttle cable had to be thawed out with a cigarette lighter.

As they progressed the weather improved, and they reached Dieppe in time for a ferry that evening. They laughed and cried and spent their last £10 on a great meal. In Portsmouth the following morning a Customs man asked, 'Where have you been?' When John reeled off more than a dozen European countries, he replied, 'I asked for that didn't I?'

John and Jane still have the Triumph – 'we couldn't get rid of it after all that'. They also decided to get married, on the theory that if they could stick that journey (and the tent). . .

It is refreshing to hear about a Bonneville like the South's, getting a good gallop. T120s used to be considered almost disposable machines which sports riders would thrash in the knowledge that plentiful replacements and cheap spares were there if you blew them up. However, with the passage of time, the Bonnie's status as a motorcycle icon, particularly for the pre-unit and late 1960s 650s, has increasingly shifted the emphasis to preserving and restoring them. This may be spurred on by the rising prices these machines command, but it is an entirely legitimate pursuit, which in the best restored examples, turns back time and allows a future generation to see exactly what all the fuss was about. Despite the Bonneville's increasing value however, all the restorers we met also ride their machines.

Restoration requires its own set of very precise skills, as well as an extraordinary persistence, as admirable in its way as the nerve a rocker needed to keep a pre-unit's power on at any cost through those deceptive bends. **John Vernon**, for instance, the owner of the beautiful 1959 and '61 T120s depicted in Chapter 2, was driven to find out how the factory had originally achieved the finish on their carburettors, so that he could replicate it. On machines that were to be raced, he found the carbs were painted opalescent silver, but on the stock bikes at that time, the carb body's unique frosty look was achieved by turning them in a barrel with a mixture of aggregate and a special fluid – hence the 'fingers' of run on original examples. If knowledge like this is not sought out and recorded, very soon it is gone for good.

One of Britain's top Bonneville restorers is **Graham Bowen**, owner of the stunning, award-winning 1968 T120 and '70 T120RT shown in Chapter 3. Graham is a private individual, not a professional, commercial restorer, but his machines put a lot of the latters' efforts to shame. They are the result of focus so sharp it borders on obsession, although Graham is a relaxed enough individual, and luck also seems to have played a part in turning up parts. He talked first about the T120RT, the clandestine 750 put together for racing homologation in the States.

'I know of only three other T120RTs in the US, and one in England, but that's got a 650 barrel. I have another Routt barrel. In fact I think he may still be in business – I have newish boxed-up forged or cast Routt pistons in both 9.0:1 and 10.5:1. My RT has 10.5:1 compression, and petrol for it is a problem

Graham Bowen with his rare and beautifully restored T120RT.

now. I 'phoned worldwide looking for those Routt pistons, but in the end Nobby Clarke's shop had a pair on the shelf, though they did cost twice as much as Hepolites.

'The bike is almost completely original. It should feature all UNF bolts, but there are a couple of cycle thread fasteners. And the seat pan is new, but with the original cover and foam. I get transfers from the excellent VMCC scheme, but the sticker on the Lucas loom was something else. Also Lucas PUZ5A batteries are not available now, but I've got a guy who will get them for me if he finds them. And Windtone horns are very, very hard to find. In the end, someone gave me one! I'd 'phoned New Zealand, Australia, the USA and couldn't locate one. Then I was talking to a friend a mile away and he had a couple of the hooters. Both right-hand! But I had a left-hand one. I had to give my friend his back, once I'd found a right-hand one myself.

'The T120RT engine has been gone through completely, and has all original parts, bearings included. The machining and the rebore were done by John Card up here in Essex, who used to race Triumphs in the early Seventies. For cycle parts, for the right look, original tin-ware

Graham is a patient, meticulous man, and it pays off.

is important. But Cliff Rushworth at Ace Classics in East London goes to a lot of bother to get things right. His gaiter clips for instance are very old ones, dead right except for not having the part numbers stamped on them. I found a couple of genuine new/old stock ones, and used a combination of the two. But the thing with the parts is, being on the network. People know I'm after something and look out for it, and I do the same for them. It works for bike details too. At the Stafford classic show, Cliff Rushworth introduced me to John Healy, a veteran Triumph dealer from Massachusetts, and looking at my T120RT, he said there shouldn't be washers for the outside of the top of the rear suspension units. That doesn't show on contemporary photographs.

'The '68 T120 was my first go, and there are one or two bits I would change now. It was a transition bike as far as UNF bolts went. I didn't do the engine's bottom end myself, and there's a little whine on the layshaft bearing. It niggles me. And the petrol tank has a tiny leak, though it only does it when the tank's bolted in place. The brake plates were always cast aluminium. They come back from the States painted black – whole engines do too, sometimes. I clean the brake plates by water-blasting, not bead-blasting, and now they're so damn clean they discolour very quickly!

'To be honest, out of all my bikes, the best to ride isn't a Bonnie at all, it's a 1967 650 single carb TR6. But it's not as angry as a Bonneville, and it doesn't go as quick.'

In the end, though the Bonnie's true glory days may have been on the dirt tracks and deserts of America, or smoking off fast cars down at the local A&W, the T120 was 'Made in England'. And specifically in the Coventry area, which has its own very particular traditions of craftsmanship and labour organisation. While Birmingham had been a centre of industry for over a century, Coventry, although it already had a long tradition of industrial skills and organised labour, only really started to grow in 1937–8, expanding with the aircraft and motor industry. Despite the punishing Blitz, it mushroomed during the Second World War. It was known post-war for high wages and labour militancy, but the tradition of pride in craftsmanship was never lost.

So it is appropriate that the acknowledged top restorer of Triumph twins, **Hughie Hancox**, should be Coventry born and bred. Hughie joined the Triumph Engineering Co at Meriden in 1953 and worked there, apart from a spell of National Service riding TRW twins with the Royal Signals White Helmets display team, until the workers' blockade of Meriden began in 1973. His time in the Repair Shop, as a tester with the Experimental Department, and as a staff member with Service gave him a uniquely comprehensive knowledge of Meriden's post-war twins. Hughie lives in the past, and relishes it. A keen Second World War aviation buff, his restoration work takes place in part of an old factory which he shares with son-in-law John Critchlow, the expert on Triumph paint matches, and which now belongs to the Sikh Temple. He works to a fat soundtrack of 1940's big band dance music from Xavier Cugat, Glen Miller and the Andrews Sisters. On the wall there's a fading poster of a T100 Daytona with Percy Tait in the saddle smiling down, and Hughie chuckles as he remembers the time when Triumph's ace rider was returning to his farm in his van with a pig he had bought at auction, which then had a litter in the back… Hughie is Coventry and Triumph, through and through.

'This building went up in 1908; it's where the first Coventry Challenge light cars were made, as well as Challenge motorcycles and bicycles. There are still hessian-bound hooks in the ceiling where they used to hang components up. We're only about three quarters of a mile from the old Triumph factory in Priory Street. I remember walking with my mother down Foleshill Road, outside here, on the morning after the big Blitz night, with the cobbled wooden blocks from the road blown into piles everywhere, and tram lines twisted up in the air like liquorice. When I started work, one of my first jobs was shuttling back and forth from Priory Street to Meriden, fetching ex-WD stuff from the bombed-out factory, mainly 3H engines, gearboxes and forks – the long boxes of girder forks had often been used to block up holes and windows – and taking it back to Meriden, mostly for sale to dealers. Strange.

'I've got two Bonnevilles in for restoration at present. One's a '61. The guy first gave me the engine and gearbox to rebuild six years ago. Then later he decided I should do it all, he didn't have the time. He'd bought it in bits, with the swinging-arm and frame already powder-coated. It looked OK when he wheeled it in, but everything was only loosely hung together. So we had to strip it right down. We give a guarantee with all our work, and we can't guarantee what we haven't seen. We found the swinging-arm and frame had all been powder-coated in one piece – and the swinging-arm was solid, it wouldn't move at all. We had to fit a new one.

'So we dismantled and checked everything, including the wheels, even though they had been done. You can't take anything for granted, because your name is going to be on the bike and you want to be certain. We found stuff like one of the brakes with only one brake shoes spring, and on the other the shoe had a chunk

out of it. We listed the spares we would need. For engine spares I use Sean at Hamrax and Matt Holder's Velocette company, which is trade only, in the old Triumph No 2 building. Today, only cycle parts are hard to get, and now Ace Classics are getting to grips with that. I can get a rear mudguard off Cliff there, and I can guarantee that it will fit. Mudguard splitting was more with the unit engines, as well as tanks. The worst of the vibes in the pre-unit seemed to only effect the electrical system, ie headlamp bulbs with their filaments shaken off.

'This bike has the optional rev-counter take-off on the timing case – you could specify it on build, but Triumph also did CPs, (carton packs), including one with a tacho kit. As a '61 it will be Silver Sheen and Sky Blue. I don't know about echoing the sky at Bonneville, but I know it was the Yanks who dictated the pastel colours. There was also another connotation on the Sky Blue; somebody likened it to the Spitfire's Duck Egg blue underside.

'This '61 had the usual problem with the eight-stud head of cracking, from inboard of the stud hole to the valve seats. We machined out the originals, welded the head and reshaped the hemisphere, then made sure the head was true and hadn't been distorted by the welding before cutting the main seats. Then we heated the head, froze the new inserts with nitrogen which were suitable for use with unleaded fuel, and fitted them with a 7–10 thou interference fit. It's complicated because you can't just weld the head; some try to vee out the crack and weld down it, but the arc behaves in a funny way, it fetches the alloy away from the seat and you end up with a gap between the edge of the seat and the aluminium. You have to machine out the seat first.

'Another pre-unit problem, and this bike has got it, is the gearbox working loose in the bottom ½in mounting. The same through-bolt goes through the rear frame and the bottom gearbox lug, and the gearbox faces wear, where the long stud goes through. After that, even though you tighten it up, it doesn't nip the gearbox up if there's play there, so the bottom of the gearbox is jumping about.

'It's a common fault. At Meriden we had a

Hughie Hancox on the bike he uses as daily transport – a Triumph of course – a Tiger Cub.

Hughie at his workbench, with a pre-unit 650 in for treatment.

little spreader, a Trophy fork pinch nut and ⅜in bolt, which would spread the bottom of the frame apart until you could slip a ½in plain washer in there. Line the washer up, let the spreader off, and the frame would clamp up and take all the slop out of the bottom of the gearbox. Just a little trick. I've also got a shock-absorber sleeve with the top half of a kick-start welded on to it, and you can slot it over the end of the crankshaft, and use it to turn the motor over when you are timing. That's ex-Meriden, and so is this set of stud drives. You see that rack of rusty tanks over there? They're from the Meriden cellar. See how each one has been punctured in the side in the same way? That

was workers' co-op guys during the sit-in …

'The other Bonnie we're doing is a '72 oil-in-frame 650. I swore I'd never do one of those, only the guy came in with a Tesco bag full of money! And some people swear by them. This one was quite well sorted. It had been used since 1990 – basically it's just the frame and centre-stand which need work. The stops for the stands let go on the frame, and then the stands go way further back than they should and you have a hell of a job to get the bike on and off them. You have to weld on a pair of brackets between the frame tubes and the stand's pivot ears. Also the top tank bolt bracket has cracked, so it's being welded too.

Alex Scobie (in the saddle, left) with Edward Turner at the high-speed Montlhéry launch of the Bonnie's forebear, the 650 Thunderbird.

'I don't like the oil-in-frames basically because of their connotations. I remember my friend the late Alex Scobie going to a preview launch of the '71 range at Umberslade Hall. Alex with his bristling moustache, steely eyes and his pipe, had been one of the riders who lapped Montlhéry in 1949 at 90mph for 500 miles, for the launch of the Thunderbird. He'd road-tested the GP Triumph racer at full speed on the old A45, and he knew as much about motorcycles as anyone I ever met. At Umberslade he walked round the P39-framed Bonneville, pointing with his pipe stem at duff features and saying, 'This isn't going to work … this isn't going to work …', until someone took him by the arm and walked him away hissing, "Keep your bloody mouth shut!" It was too late for them to stop it all by then.'

The Forties' music was still playing as I left, thinking what a long and winding road it was that had led from the dazzling white Utah salt flats to a post-industrial city in the new millennium. But the Bonneville, in all its guises, had ridden that road like an angry streak of chrome and defiance, taut, nervy, demanding and pared to the bone, with a rasping, roaring whirr of engine song shouting nothing but 'Ride Hard or Stay Home'.

And in our hearts and minds, in our oil-stained souls, the Bonneville rides that highway yet.

New Millennium Bonneville

Serendipity, the art of happy accident, does sometimes feature in the otherwise hard-nosed world of the professional writer. The fact that a new Triumph Bonneville should be launched just two months before the publication of this book celebrating the old Bonnie, seemed like something of a grace note.

From 1990, John Bloor's Hinckley-based Triumph company at first took some pains to distance themselves from the poor reputation of the later Meriden Triumph products. Only late in 1994, once a reputation for solidly engineered modern motorcycles had been established, and with Hinckley's serious penetration of the US market beginning via their subsidiary Triumph Motorcycles America Ltd, the company began to capitalize on the legendary legacy of their name in the motorcycle world.

Some of the retro efforts, notably the inappropriately named Adventurer which was said to be the particular baby of the boss, were less than happy. But the Thunderbird triple, while very much based on the existing product, proved both a pleasant cruiser, and a successful one. After the rights to the Bonneville name had been sorted out with the American automotive industry, a more ambitious, all-new heritage project got underway for the revival of the most resonant name of them all. It was also timed to coincide with the completion of new Triumph's second factory, half a mile from the first one. The new Bonneville was planned to be a major component in doubling the company's production, to match the 50,000-plus annual output of their European rivals, BMW. The new bike, like the original, was also to be very much US-orientated.

The development timetable for the new model began in April 1997. The outlines soon emerged: a twin-cylinder bike with a traditional 360-degree crank, pistons rising and falling together to give the required feel and sound. Fuel injection was rejected in favour of twin 36mm carburettors, traditional again but with absolutely modern throttle position sensors and electric anti-frost heaters.

That, in fact, is the theme throughout the new Bonneville – a traditional format which subtly incorporates necessary modern technology. That oversquare (86 x 68mm) twin-cylinder 790cc engine for instance, may be oil/air-cooled, and feature an oil-drain tube at the front of the engine which resembles the old twins' pushrod tube, but it also benefits from a tactfully concealed frame-mounted oil cooler, and internally, from chain-driven twin-overhead camshafts, and 4-valve cylinder heads with twin plugs – to help meet emission standards for California, the epicentre in terms of both the style and the market for the bike. The motor

The new Bonnie steers excellently.

Triumph's heritage was the key concept for the Hinckley Bonneville.

also features twin balancer shafts, so traditional vibes should be stimulating rather than punishing. The engine is wet sump so there is no need for an oil tank.

The styling cues, in fact, derive from that peak T120 model year of 1969, from the gold-lined Scarlet Red and Silver two-tone paint job (there's a Forest Green and Silver alternative), to the twin-shock rear end with chromed external spring units adjustable for preload only, from Kayaba, who also supply the non-adjustable 41mm front forks, which are set out at a 61° steering head angle very close to that of the original.

A few places where they haven't managed the trad look include the right-side drive chain, dictated by a gearbox derived from the T500's, modified to 5-speed and reversed, so as to allow the traditional layout of a small triangular engine cover on the right and larger clutch case on the left. The massive single disc, twin-caliper brakes, 310mm front/255mm rear, are another (welcome) innovation. Less happy to my eyes is the kink in the rear of the exhaust, no doubt dictated by the engine layout and the need for ground clearance. The tubular steel

spine frame may have twin downtubes, rather than the traditional Meriden single tube, but with the box-section swinging-arm pivotting through the crankcases, there shouldn't be any 'instant whip'! And a height for its well-padded seat of just 30.5 inches should mean no 'tall trouble' either. At 451lb dry, though, the bike is some 90lb heavier than the originals.

Preliminary reports of riding the Bonnie have been very positive. Hinckley's stated intentions were to produce an enjoyable, good looking, practical machine with lively performance, pleasant power characteristics and excellent handling, and all indicators are that they have succeeded. The engine in its present form may produce just 61bhp @ 7,400rpm, similar to many Harley-Davidsons, but there is clearly a lot of scope for tuning (think 90bhp), and more importantly the Bonnie's motor offers 90 per cent of its available torque from as low as 2,750rpm – a recipe for great low and mid-range acceleration. The days of Bonnie v Sportster shootouts may be with us again! Meanwhile, let's wish the best of British luck to this hopeful-looking silicone chip off the grand old block.

Appendix:
Engine and frame numbers

Triumph Bonneville engine and frame numbers were matched, so they usually correspond. Until 1969, the numbers consisted of a prefix, ie T120, and were sometimes followed by model designation letters, and concluded with the actual (usually five-figure) number.

Model years usually ran from late August/early September of the preceding year, to mid-August in the model year itself. Early Bonneville frame numbers could carry an 'S' prefix to denote swinging-arm; and then, from mid-season in 1960, started again at 101 and until the end of the 1962 season carried a 'D' prefix, indicating the duplex downtube frame. For the 1963 model year, with unit construction, the numbers began again at 101, this time with a 'DU' prefix.

The Bonneville designation letters which followed the prefix were as follows:

Letter	Year	Model
A	1960 only	USA road
B	1960 only	USA/competition/street scrambler
R	1961 – on	USA road
C	1961 – on	USA/competition/street scrambler
TT	Mid-1966–7	USA TT Specials
RT	1970 only	USA limited run 750
V	1973 – on	Five-speed gearbox

E	1978 – on	Emission control
D	1979–80	Special
ES	Mid-1980 – on	Electric start
AV	1981 – on	Anti-vibration
LE	1982	Royal (Wedding) limited edition
TSS	1982–3	Eight-valve
TSX	1982–3	Factory custom

Engine/frame numbers

1959	Pre-unit	020076-029363
1960	Pre-unit	029364-030424, then D101-D7726
1961	Pre-unit	D7727-D15788
1962	Pre-unit	D15789-D20308
1963	Unit 650	DU101-DU5824
1964	Unit 650	DU5825-DU13374
1965	Unit 650	DU13375-DU24874
1966	Unit 650	DU24875-DU44393
1967	Unit 650	DU44394-DU66245
1968	Unit 650	DU66246-DU85903
1969	Unit 650	DU85904-DU90282

Early in the 1969 season, commencing with JC00101, an entirely new system was introduced, with a two-letter prefix for every machine, the first letter being a month code, the second letter a year code. This prefix was followed by engine numbers in series, irrespective of models. There were inconsistencies in the numbering: the unit 650 numbers had reached 36585 in January 1970, then reverted to 30001 with the start of the oil-in-frame machines. In 1981, since the coding system would begin repeating itself, a third letter (A) was included to avoid repetition.

Date code

Month	Year
A – January	C – October 1968–July 1969
B – February	D – August 1969–August 1970
C – March	E – September 1970–August 1971
D – April	G – September 1971–August 1972
E – May	H – September 1972–August 1973
G – June	J – September 1973–August 1974
H – July	K – September 1974–August 1975
J – August	N – September 1975–August 1976
K – September	P – September 1976–August 1977
N – October	X – September 1977–August 1978
P – November	A – September 1978–August 1979
X – December	B – September 1979–August 1980
	DA – September 1980–January 1982
	EA – February 1982-3

1970	Unit 650	JD24849–ND60540
1971	Unit 650	NE01436–HE30869
1972	Unit 650	HG30870–JG?
1973	Unit 724cc	JH15435–XH22018
	Unit 747cc	XH22019–GH36466
	Unit 650	JH15366–GH?
1974	Unit 750	GJ55101–NJ60032
	Unit 650	GJ5510 –KJ59067
1975	Unit 750	- to EK62239
	Unit 650	- to NJ60070

NB The 1974 and 1975 numbers refer to machines released for sale by the Meriden co-operative during those years.

1976	Unit 750	HN62501 –GN72283
1977	Unit 750	GP75000–JP84931
1978	Unit 750	HX00100–HX10747

This number was followed by XB24609 to XB24790, as 182 twins were mistakenly marked with letter 'B'.

1979	Unit 750	HA11001–KA24999
1980	Unit 750	PB25001–KB27500
1981	Unit 750/650	KDA28001–DDA29427
1982	Unit 750/650	EDA30001–BDA31693
1983	Unit 750	BEA33001–AEA34393, ends
1985	Les Harris	
	Unit 750	EN000001
1987	Les Harris	
	Unit 750	SN001258, ends

NB An FFC engine number prefix, used on some models made by Meriden from Winter 1980 onwards, denoted Factory Fitted Custom, indicating built to customer's personal specification of colour and ancillaries.

Index